# SIMON COWELL

## THE UNAUTHORIZED BIOGRAPHY

# SIMON COWELL

## THE UNAUTHORIZED BIOGRAPHY

*Chas Newkey-Burden*

MICHAEL O'MARA BOOKS LIMITED

First published in Great Britain in 2009 by
Michael O'Mara Books Limited
9 Lion Yard
Tremadoc Road
London SW4 7NQ

A CIP catalogue record for this book is available from
the British Library.

Papers used by Michael O'Mara Books Limited are natural, recyclable
products made from wood grown in sustainable forests. The
manufacturing processes conform to the environmental regulations
of the country of origin.

ISBN: 978-1-84317-485-1

1 2 3 4 5 6 7 8 9 10

www.mombooks.com

Designed and typeset by e-type
Plate section designed by www.envydesign.co.uk
Cover design by www.envydesign.co.uk

Printed and bound in Great Britain by CPI Cox & Wyman,
Reading, RG1 8EX

# CONTENTS

# ACKNOWLEDGEMENTS

I would like to gratefully thank the people who kindly agreed to be interviewed for this book. Among these were numerous contestants from *Pop Idol*, *American Idol* and *The X Factor*, including Niki Evans, Anthony Fedorov, The MacDonald Brothers, Rowetta Satchell, Susanne Courtney (née Manning), Daniel de Bourg, Olly Manson, Luke Bayer and David Graham. Thanks also to Julie Burchill, Toby Young, Zeddy Lawrence, Julia Raeside and Jonathan Sacerdoti for sparing time to offer their experiences and insight.

Thanks to those who, while declining to be interviewed, nonetheless responded to my requests and wished me well with the book, including Korben and The Unconventionals. Darren Evans, Anthony Wooton and Gordon Campbell were helpful in setting up some of the aforementioned interviews. Thanks also to Justin Cohen and Frankie Genchi.

I am grateful to Michael O'Mara, Lindsay Davies, Sarah Sandland, Anna Marx, Kate Gribble and Shauna Bartlett.

Thanks to everyone who has bought any of my books. Finally, I am indebted to Simon Cowell himself, who has provided so much wonderful entertainment over the years. His own autobiography, *I Don't Mean to Be Rude, But...*, was an invaluable source for some of the earlier passages of this book, but I hope that by bringing his story up to date I have done justice to the man behind the formidable entertainment machine.

This book is dedicated to Chris – my very own outspoken, dark, handsome Englishman. To borrow a Cowellism: you are a gentleman, sir.

# Picture credits

Page 1: Mirrorpix (top); © Paul Kramer/The Sun (centre); Mirrorpix (bottom)

Page 2: © Alpha (top); © Jeff Spicer/Alpha (bottom)

Page 3: Dave Hogan/Getty Images (top); Patrick Rideaux/Rex Features (bottom)

Page 4: Capital Pictures (top); © Jeff Spicer/Alpha (bottom)

Page 5: ShowBizIreland/Getty Images (top); Jonathan Hordle/Rex Features (bottom)

Page 6: Mirrorpix (top); Capital Pictures (bottom)

Page 7: © Kate Green/Alpha (top); Cruisepictures/EMPICS/PA Images (bottom)

Page 8: © Austin Young

Page 9: Henry Lamb/BEI/Rex Features (top); Dave Hogan/Getty Images (bottom)

Page 10: Dave Hogan/Getty Images (top); bigpicturesphoto.com (bottom)13

Page 11: Dan Wooller/WireImage/Getty Images (top); © Penny Lancaster, supplied by Alpha (bottom)

Page 12: BDG/Rex Features (top); Brian Rasic/Rex Features (centre); Gregory Pace/BEI/Rex Features (bottom)

Page 13: Jim Smeall/BEI/Rex Features (top); Ken McKay/Rex Features (centre); Ken McKay/Rex Features (bottom)

Page 14: ITV/Rex Features (top); ITV/Rex Features (centre); Richard Young/Rex Features (bottom)

Page 15: Ian West/PA Wire/PA Images (top); Ken McKay/Rex Features (bottom)

Page 16: celebritypictures.co.uk

# INTRODUCTION

'Excuse me,' said the middle-aged diner in the American restaurant as he approached a famous fellow diner's table, 'if I pay you a hundred thousand dollars, will you stand in our bedroom and insult me as I make love to my wife?' This is not the sort of request most people would expect to receive from a stranger, but then Simon Cowell is not like most people.

He has become globally recognized for the frank verdicts he delivers to contestants on televison talent shows like *The X Factor* and *American Idol*, so much so that 'Cowell' has become a byword for blunt honesty. Thanks to the success of these shows and some of the artists they have launched, he has also become incredibly rich, and his ambition shows no sign of abating. When once asked what he wants most in the world, he said with characteristic candour: 'Money. As much money as I can get my hands on.' He's getting his hands on plenty: his personal fortune is estimated to be in excess of £100 million.

Cowell's ascent to such heady heights has taken an unlikely route. His journey to the top of the celebrity tree is in stark contrast to those of the numerous well-known sports stars who spent their childhoods slaving away to perfect their technique, or the actors and singers who endured humourless years being coached by bossy teachers at stage school and pushy parents at home. These budding stars were led to believe that years of exhausting hard work was the *only* way to achieve those two prized commodities: fame and fortune.

Neither does Cowell's life follow the familiar entrepreneurial narrative of the kid from the impoverished background whose hunger drove him to extraordinary business success.

Fame came late and suddenly to Cowell. He was unknown at forty-two, nationally infamous by the time he turned forty-three and internationally famous only a few years later. Prior to that he had four decades during which there were only occasional clues as to what the future held. He had a joyful childhood, which he spent rebelling at school and playing ever more devious and hilarious practical jokes at home. His was a happy household that echoed with laughter, and his family was financially comfortable, so Cowell couldn't be said to have an inherent hunger for wealth.

Professionally, Cowell's career started slowly. In his twenties he had some success in the music business and lapped up the glamorous perks and lifestyle that came with it. But then he lost everything, and at thirty was forced, rather ignominiously, to move back to his parents' home. What spurred him on, waking up under his parents' roof, to become one of the most driven, successful and famous men on the planet? The man named, in a 2008 poll of children, as *the* most famous person in the world, finishing ahead of even the Queen and God? Where did he derive the confidence to be so unflinchingly frank on television? And what is the truth about Cowell's much-speculated-upon love life?

Cowell is a man of paradoxes: a straight-talking judge with a cruel tongue but a kind heart. A wealthy man from comfortable stock, he nonetheless has the common touch and is unflinchingly generous. Handsome and charismatic, only one of his romantic relationships has lasted longer than a few years.

*X Factor* finalist Niki Evans, one of many contestants interviewed for this book, saw some of Cowell's contrasts close-up: 'He's a loveable rogue,' she smiles. 'He's a mummy's boy, but very ruthless. If he wants something he'll get it. Make no mistake about that. He's a hard man with a heart, that's what he is. People will be shocked to learn about the real Simon Cowell.'

Here is his story...

# CHAPTER ONE

# A CHEEKY CHILDHOOD

S imon Cowell first showed his ability to deliver a shapely put-down at an early age. One Christmas Day, his mother Julie had spent special time and care getting herself ready for lunch. With her extravagant clothes, neatly styled hair and carefully applied make-up all complete, she donned a large white fur hat and strode down the stairs of the family home. She asked her son what he thought of her outfit.

'Mum,' replied Simon, 'you look like a poodle.' He was four years of age.

Cowell was born in Brighton, Sussex, on 7 October 1959, but soon afterwards his family moved to Elstree in Hertfordshire. His date of birth makes him a Libran, a sign associated with the trait of narcissism. He's a believer in astrology, once declaring, 'If I'm sitting in a restaurant and I'm facing a wall, I can't enjoy myself. I'm a Libran and I have the stereotypical Libran characteristic: everything has to look nice.'

His father, Eric Cowell, was a successful estate agent and quantity surveyor, while his mother, Josie Dalglish, known as Julie, was a glamorous socialite with a background in theatre (her stage name was Julie Brett). The couple met on the train to Birmingham – a route they both travelled regularly – but it took two years of shared journeys before Eric plucked up the courage to speak to the attractive lady he had admired from afar. They went for a drink and began dating, and before long they were married.

They were a glamorous couple: Eric was handsome and suave with striking black hair; Julie was slim and beautiful with a natural class and elegance. Between them they already had four children from previous relationships, three boys – Tony, John and Michael – and a girl called June. They were keen to have a child together, but following complications their first son, Stephen, died a week after his birth. Julie then suffered further heartbreak with two miscarriages.

Finally, she fell pregnant again. 'I remember being absolutely petrified all the way through the pregnancy,' she told the *Daily Mail*. 'I bled quite badly three or four months in, and I was in hospital. I was sure it would go wrong.' This time, though, everything was fine and she gave birth to a baby boy called Simon. Keen to keep him in good health, she made sure baby Simon had plenty of fresh air, often leaving him outside in his pink pram. Sometimes Tony, who is nine years older than Simon, would push his little brother up and down the street in the pram. 'It was the 1960s and everything was a sort of pink then,' Tony recalled. 'I found that if I pushed him really fast, swerving in and out along the pavement, he laughed. The faster I went, the more he laughed. He was about two. Simon's very into speed and fast cars now. We reckon that was his introduction to it.'

Eric and Julie brought up Simon alongside his three half

brothers, his half sister and his brother Nicholas, who was born two years after Simon. Both Cowell's birthplace and childhood stomping ground are entirely fitting surroundings for the man that he became. Brighton is a city synonymous with thrills, entertainment and the pursuit of unashamed pleasure, while Elstree was a Hertfordshire village steeped in showbusiness during the Swinging Sixties when Cowell was growing up. Nowadays, he spends several months each year in Los Angeles, rubbing shoulders with the cream of Hollywood at exclusive parties. It's little wonder Cowell feels so at home in such circumstances and surroundings, for during the 1960s Elstree was Britain's equivalent of Tinseltown, thanks to the presence of two major film studios.

The most prestigious of these was the Elstree Film Studios, which were built in the 1920s at the behest of a young British film producer called Herbert Wilcox and his Hollywood contact J.D. Williams. The legendary Alfred Hitchcock used the studios, and it soon became a mainstay of the British cinema industry. By the 1960s, when the Cowells moved into the area, the studios were also being used by the television industry, with shows such as *The Saint* and *The Avengers* being shot there. Consequently, the suburban village of Elstree became a bubbly celebrity haunt where a galaxy of stars used to come to work and party, including Bette Davis, Roger Moore and Gregory Peck. Expensive cars were seen on the village lanes, famous faces were glimpsed through windows, and at night champagne corks could be heard popping at posh parties.

The Cowell family moved into a nineteenth-century, eight-bedroom home in Barnet Lane called Abbots Mead, which was one of the best homes in the area. Set in fives acres of private woodland, it was a grand building from the outside, but internally it was in some disarray and took Eric the best part of two years to restore.

The family's nearest neighbour was Gerry Blatner, who was the head of Warner Brothers Films in the United Kingdom and outrageously well-connected in the world of cinema. When Hollywood's great and good were in town, they all visited Blatner's home, guaranteeing excitement in the Cowell household as the stars pulled up next door to party. The first big name they remember seeing was Bette Davis, who was spotted, quite literally over the garden fence by Julie.

Soon this sort of incident became commonplace for the village's newest residents and the Cowells weren't overwhelmed by the glamour for long. Eric looked not unlike a film star himself with his handsome, debonair appearance, and the elegant Julie had experience as an accomplished dancer and actress on the London stage. As such, they fitted in perfectly with Elstree's showbusiness royalty, and were soon throwing parties at home with their own star-studded guest lists.

Simon was also busy blending in. He sat on Bette Davis's knee as she learned her script; watched Roger Moore recording *The Saint* and hitched a ride round the studios with his brother Tony, who had found work there as a runner. However, one encounter with a famous face proved less satisfactory. Cowell recalls approaching British actor Bernard Cribbins for an autograph and having his request turned down. It was a moment that had a big influence on how Cowell treats such requests today, as we shall see.

Cowell was far from intimidated by his famous neighbours, and even enjoyed treating them to some of his cutting punchlines. When asked by actor Trevor Howard whether he wanted to be a thespian one day, Cowell simply yawned and replied, 'No, I don't like actors.' What a little charmer.

He did, however, like music. Well, some of it anyway. The first record he ever owned was 'She Loves You' by The Beatles, which was released in the UK on 23 August 1963. It wasn't just the Fab Fours' music that captured young Cowell's attention. He also admired their rock and roll lifestyle of fast cars, champagne, parties and doting young women. One day, he thought. He has since said that he wished he was working in the music industry in the 1960s so he could have been the man that signed The Beatles.

Much as Cowell loved the Fab Four as a boy, he was ever the critic and was very outspoken about music he *didn't* like. This included the songs of jazz and swing singers such as Frank Sinatra, Charles Aznavour and Shirley Bassey, all of whom his parents loved (he has since become a major fan of Sinatra, however).

Back then, he became so frustrated by his parents' musical tastes that he hid their records, and even, on one particular occasion, grabbed a screwdriver and inflicted a vicious scratch on one of his mother's favourite albums. This wasn't his only moment of musical anarchy. He once disrupted a music class at school by banging the bass drum he was playing with such volume that he drowned out the rest of the ensemble. His teacher, Mrs Jones, was not amused.

\*

At home Cowell continued to be inspired by the famous people who visited his neighbours. When his parents threw lavish parties, young Simon would peek down at proceedings from the top of the staircase and dream of moving in similar circles. Then, in the morning, he would watch his father hop into his iconic E-type white Jaguar, pop a fat cigar in his mouth and speed off to work. It was an impressive sight, and Cowell couldn't help but admire his father's style.

While Eric was hard at work in London, however, Cowell could be a proper menace at home. He was a cheeky little scamp to the family's nanny, Heather, and his mother continued to come in for criticism. Having compared her to a poodle when he was four years old, three years later Cowell told her she looked like a canary.

Another favourite pastime of Cowell's was to cause mischief for his younger sibling Nicholas, which mostly consisted of blaming Nicholas for the naughty things he had done himself. Other cheeky tricks he played on Nicholas included tormenting him with the upsetting news that Father Christmas was not real 'and the quicker you come to terms with it, the better', and inflicting a distinctly average haircut on him. When Julie spotted Nicholas with his disastrous crop, she was in no doubt at all as to who was responsible, and her scream could be heard all round the large house: 'Where's Simon?' Nicholas admits, however, that he was hardly an angel himself. As he later recalled: 'I guess we were the two brats of the family.'

Cowell's cousin Penny Christopher recalled in *Heat* magazine an occasion when the young Cowell interrupted a breakfast in bed she was enjoying at their house by running into her bedroom and saying, 'When I go to bed, I wear pyjamas. Why don't you?'

The brats were in particularly mischief-making form at older brother Michael's wedding in the late 1960s. There, the ten-year-old Cowell had his first taste of being tipsy after cheekily pinching the adult guests' wine. 'As soon as a glass was put down on a table, Simon would neck it back,' Michael told the *Sunday Mirror*. 'At one point he pushed the bridesmaid, who was about eight, into the swimming pool. Our mum had to dive in and save her. She was furious as she was totally soaked in her posh dress. Simon then slunk off with our younger brother Nicholas – his partner in crime – and got my dog obliterated by feeding it wine. He then changed all the place settings round so he was sitting on the top table. It was an utter nightmare. My wife wasn't impressed.'

It wasn't the first time Cowell's devilish side had caused rifts in his brother's love life. Years earlier, as a teenager, Michael brought his first girlfriend back to the family home. As Michael sat nervously on the sofa with his girl, trying to enjoy some privacy, Cowell burst into the room carrying a pornographic magazine in his hand. He passed the magazine to his brother and said, 'Thanks for the loan, Mike.'

Another favourite trick was to put notices in the windows of Elstree's shops advertizing 'French lessons' and 'a big chest for sale', together with the family's telephone number. It was left to Julie to field the resulting flood of phone calls from interested local men. Another time, on the day of an important board meeting at Eric's office, Cowell swapped the handkerchief in his father's suit pocket for a pair of his mother's knickers. No wonder his brother

Tony said that Cowell made his home seem like the set of the horror film *The Omen*.

He was also a brat outside of the family home. One day, the twelve-year-old Cowell was feeling bored during a tiresome suburban bus journey when he had a brainwave for a bit of mischief. He had a pea-shooter in his pocket – an essentially harmless 'weapon' made out of plastic and capable of doing nothing more threatening than firing a dry pea for a distance of five yards. However, to a bus driver trying to concentrate on the road, it could easily pass for a real gun – and it did. So when Cowell pointed the peashooter at the driver and told him, 'This is a hijack – take me to Watford!' the poor man took the threat at face value and didn't pause at any subsequent stops, even when potential passengers were waiting. Cowell soon had some explaining to do to Her Majesty's police.

There was a further brush with the law when Cowell joy-rode a car at Elstree Studios and smashed it into a wall. Years later, he returned to the studios when a plaque was erected there in honour of his childhood connection with the area. 'I'm so grateful for what you've all done today,' he said at the ceremony. 'I'm honoured and very flattered. Growing up in Elstree was amazing; it was like having a slice of Hollywood on your doorstep.'

As the Sixties gave way to the Seventies, Cowell became hungry for a slice of the financial cake. True, he was a cheeky brat, but he was also ambitious. That quality – which gave him such energy and motivation later in life – was honed on the streets and lanes of Elstree. Just as Cowell's imagination was fired up by the showbiz parties his parents and neighbours threw, so he began to develop a taste for the thrill of making money. He and his siblings weren't simply handed pocket money by their parents – they had to earn it. 'We might not have had money worries, but I was concerned about the boys growing up thinking everything would come to them on a plate,' recalled Julie in an interview with the *Daily Mail*. 'I remember Simon moaning once: "She's got me working on a farm, picking stones." He hated it. Of course they didn't need to work, but I felt it was important that they get out there and learn that money doesn't grow on trees. No child of mine was going to be spoiled.' It's tough lessons like these that helped mould Cowell into the astonishingly driven man he has become.

In addition to performing the required tasks to earn his pocket money, Cowell found ways to earn further funds beyond the family home. At just eight years of age he had a successful local car-cleaning business, from which he could make up to £10 a day. This was good money for a boy his age in the 1960s. His childhood was proving to be a combination of the two things that would later dominate Cowell's life: money and celebrity. He was in his element being surrounded by movie stars and full of energy finding ways to make money, and with money came more independence than most lads his age could dream of. The many jobs he took during his school years included spells as a window cleaner, babysitter and carol singer. One hopes that his carol singing efforts weren't met with the sort of withering verdict he became famous for later in life.

Above all Cowell was happy. 'I loved having my own money,' he recalled. 'In school holidays I would apply for jobs in warehouses, petrol stations or on a farm – I was always happier working than just mucking around.' With the extra funds came all manner of benefits, including increased independence and more success with girls. 'We were the sort of boys who were always making things happen, coming up with schemes to make a bit of cash, or to get girls,' recalled his brother Nicholas.

After starting his first business at the age of eight, Cowell passed another rite of passage the following year with his first kiss. During a garden party at his home, he played spin-the-bottle with some other youngsters and was paired for a kiss with a local girl called Tara. 'It was very cute,' recalled Tara McDonald-Smith in 2008. 'It was my first kiss, too, so I will never forget it. It was very innocent and easy. We didn't know what we were doing, but it was a great experience for both of us, it was very memorable.' Asked what the boyhood Cowell was like, McDonald-Smith confirmed that he was similar to the present-day version. 'He always said what was on his mind. I wouldn't have said he was a shy boy, let's put it this way.'

Cowell was growing up fast. Having had his first kiss at nine, at the age of ten he began smoking cigarettes – a habit he maintains to this day. He and Tony would pinch their father's posh Sobranie cigarettes and puff away in secret. From then on, he said, 'All of my school was about cigarettes.'

Cowell was proving a precocious child, much in awe of his older brother and keen to be considered a contemporary, despite their nine-year age gap. Consequently he found school an enormously inconvenient bore and was deeply unimpressed by what the world of education had to offer. During an interview with the entertainment website parade.com, Cowell said, 'I was always bored [at school]. I didn't like the rules and I didn't like discipline. So when someone said to me, "These are the best days of your life," I actually thought about jumping off a bridge. I was like, "If it gets any worse than this I'm done," because I hated school.'

He attended Radlett Prep School, an independent day school in substantial grounds near Kendal Wood in Hertfordshire. He resented the disciplined air of school and was terribly bored by most lessons, though he did enjoy English and art classes, and sports like athletics and football.

He must have been disruptive, as within a few months of joining the school, Cowell's parents received a warning from the headmaster that he was planning to expel their son. His mother recalls Cowell becoming an increasing handful at home around this time, too, and in the end he was sent away to board at Dover College. Founded in September 1871, the school is set in grand grounds in Dover, Kent. At around the time he joined, the school went from being all-boys' to co-educational, a development Cowell heartily approved in theory but was disappointed by in practice, primarily because of the quantity and quality of the female intake. The few girls that did join were guaranteed attention from the hordes of teenage boys at the school, but Cowell feels that this was due to general male adolescent lustiness rather than the attractiveness of the girls. 'I expect they had a rude awakening later on in their lives,' he quipped in his book *I Don't Mean to Be Rude, But...*

Not the politest of judgements. The former assistant housemaster of Dover College, Lorenzo Smerillo gave his own verdict on Cowell in *The Guardian* in 2008. 'Simon was a very unhappy, nicotine-addicted, skinny, scruffy, dishevelled, pimply teen – rather like most boys at any school,' said Smerillo. 'I found him amusing in a quirky way. He quite often had some wisecrack or other on the tip of his tongue.' The skinny, scruffy Cowell was far from pleased to be sent away from home and recalls with horror how, on his arrival, he went to put his trunk into storage, knowing it was the last he would see of it until the end of term. He describes the school as akin to Hogwarts in the Harry Potter stories. There was more discipline than at his previous school, which led the teenage Cowell to feel even more stifled. He sent typically melodramatic adolescent letters home, saying that he hoped his parents were happy in their warm house while he sat starving in a freezing dormitory. His return home at the end of term was swiftly followed by a scathing school report in the mail. Cowell was summoned to his father's study for a ticking off but the pair ended up bursting out laughing.

He was a rebellious pupil and enjoyed slipping away to the local pub for a drink and a smoke. When a telltale prefect spotted Cowell and some friends in their local, he reported them to the headmaster. Cowell was ordered to reveal the identities of his fellow drinkers, and when he refused he was suspended for five weeks. It was a 'punishment' that delighted Cowell, who considered it a joyous holiday from school, which he believed to be a complete waste of time. 'Every time I sat in a chemistry lesson I thought, What am I doing this for?' he said during an interview with *The Observer*. 'I don't ever want to be in a job that involves a Bunsen burner.' Like many who went on to excel in their chosen field, the young Cowell decided early on that school was an obstacle rather than anything helpful. 'I hated school,' he said. 'I thought it was a punishment. [I was] very lippy, always had an opinion.' Cowell reluctantly returned to school after his suspension and eventually left at sixteen with two O Level passes in English Language and English Literature.

His education wasn't over, though, as he was sent to technical college in Windsor to retake the O Levels he'd failed. Here, in the regal surroundings of the plush Berkshire countryside and the shadow of Windsor Castle, he passed an additional O Level in Sociology. To make money, he worked as a waiter at the ABC restaurant in the evenings. 'It was terrible. I caught the chef doing something unspeakable with a turkey once,' he recalled in the *Mirror*. 'But I was good and earned tips for being enthusiastic and fast.'

Cowell was putting more money in his pocket and enjoying the resultant pleasures. In Windsor, it would appear the girls were more to his liking, for it was while studying there that he had his first serious girlfriend and lost his virginity. He roared up to meet the girl one evening on his motorbike, and she joined him for the short ride to a local pub. Cowell had given her the idea that he was vastly experienced between the sheets, but he was secretly extremely nervous and drank heavily during the evening in a bid to control his nerves. His girlfriend proved eager to get back to Cowell's home and get on with it, and despite his nerves he claims he performed well. However, the romance was over quickly: they split when he spotted her snogging a teacher at a party. Cowell went home devastated and endured a sleepless night as he coped with the hurt. Then he phoned her the next day and asked if he could have his crash helmet back.

\*

The outside world might have thrown some challenges at Cowell, but his family gave him a warm, tight and above all secure base. It was a household full of love, warmth and laughter, which one Cowell family member describes as being like a traditional Italian family. Simon would wake up each morning to the sound of his parents chatting and giggling – not a soundtrack many couples can provide for their children on a daily basis after twenty years together. The importance of this in shaping Cowell cannot be overestimated. His confident and secure persona was formed right there in his childhood years. As we will see, the strength of his parents' marriage also affected the way he went about his own romantic relationships later in life, not always to the good, as it has left him with a feeling that he could never emulate their relationship. As he told *The Observer*, 'They were both on their second marriages and [their relationship] was unbelievably happy, to the point where the superstitious side of me goes, "I couldn't follow that". They were as happy as I've ever seen two people, mainly because they never stopped talking. From the second they woke up to the second they went to bed, yak yak yak, all day long. I used to call them the chipmunks.'

While benefiting from this environment, Cowell was still a teenager and therefore something of a rebel at heart. As his teenage years rolled by, he showed little sign of becoming more sensible. He would sulk in his bedroom, smoking heavily and listening to bands like The Eagles and Fleetwood Mac at high volume. This was the late 1970s, the era of punk rock acts like the Sex Pistols and The Clash. Cowell, however, was more interested in American pop and rock acts. His musical tastes had been broadened, not least by his brother Tony, who introduced him to acts like The Beach Boys, Bob Dylan and Neil Young during smoky, sultry teenage afternoons. Cowell went to his first concert at seventeen. It was Elton John performing in Hammersmith and he recalls it as a 'brilliant' night. Who could have predicted at this point that such a directionless young man would go on to become a driven professional worth millions of pounds? Only his brother Tony seems to have caught a glimpse of the riches and happiness that lay ahead for Cowell. 'I remember going home for Sunday lunch when Simon was sixteen or seventeen,' Tony recalled. 'He looked a wreck – he had long hair and a moustache and was drinking beer out of bottles. I thought, "He's a real rebel." I remember thinking, "You're a strong-minded bloke. You know exactly what you want out of life." I knew I didn't have to worry about him.'

At this time a television show captured Cowell's attention. ITV started broadcasting *New Faces* in 1973 and it quickly became a smash-hit show. It took the genre by storm as it had a tougher edge than previous talent shows like *Opportunity Knocks*. Hopeful acts were judged by a panel, including Alan Freeman and Clive James, and their verdicts were often tough – the toughest coming from the mouth of Mickie Most. A leading record producer, Most had conjured a string of hits for acts such as The Animals and Suzi Quatro, and he wasn't afraid of giving honest feedback to *New Faces* hopefuls. Back at Abbots Mead, Cowell sat on the floor watching the show and quickly became a fan of Most. 'He was a smart guy, knew what the public wanted and wasn't interested in the art of it all,' he told *The Sunday Times* in 2003. 'He was just interested in being successful.'

Watching Most's *New Faces* peformances fired Cowell's

ambition, but even though the television judge had captured his imagination, Cowell had yet to decide what he wanted to be successful at. Previously he had dreamed of being a train or racing driver, as many boys his age would, but he felt increasingly drawn to working in the entertainment field. Having finished his year-long stint at technical college, Cowell and Eric had a 'father and son' chat one evening about what he should do next. It was clear that his parents hoped he would use his three O Levels and his ambition to make money to pursue a nice safe career in a trade such as retail or property. Cowell, however, had other ideas. After an unsuccessful job interview at Tesco, he vowed he wouldn't work in a field that required dull conformity and strict dress codes. This determination to choose his own career path came in part from the values his mother had taught him: she had told all her children that one of the keys to a successful life is to find a job that makes you happy.

It was a lesson that rang true for Cowell, who found himself facing contradictory emotions about his future. On the one hand he had been excited by the glamour of his early exposure to showbusiness and he loved the thrill of making money. But dreams of entering the entertainment industry had always been treated with suspicion and this was even more the case during the 1970s. He didn't want to follow the example of most people his age, who were either moving onto college or travelling abroad on a gap year. However, his dream of working in the movie or music industries was considered an unachievable dream. 'Particularly,' he writes, 'as I had no experience or academic qualifications, apart from an overdeveloped ego. In hindsight, I was perfectly qualified.'

Believing that his dream of working in entertainment was misguided, he tried his hand at a series of jobs that his father helped him find. The results were almost comically disastrous. First, his father drove him to Birmingham to take a two-day course in labouring. It was a rainy day, and on arrival Cowell managed 120 minutes of crunching and sloshing around a rubble-strewn building site before he threw in the towel. It was a tense drive home for both father and son. Then came the job interview at Tesco, again set up by his father. Would young Cowell interview well? What do you think? 'The guy in charge had a go at me for turning up in jeans,' he later told the *Daily Mail*. 'Maybe I shouldn't have. Who knows? But that was that. He hated me, and I hated him.' After trading insults with his interviewer, Cowell walked out. His father then arranged for him to be interviewed for a vacancy at the Civil Service. There he faced a sombre three-person panel who quickly announced that Cowell was the most unsuitable candidate they had ever interviewed. Three decades later he would be the man sitting on a panel and delivering similarly direct verdicts – with the whole country watching.

At the time, Cowell was simply relieved that he'd been spared from taking on a job as a builder or one in a boring, stale office. 'I vowed that I'd find a job where I didn't have to wear a suit and play by the rules. So I did.' Although his father's attempts to set Cowell on a career path had not borne fruit, he had instilled in his son the key qualities that would see him rise to the top of the entertainment industry: determination and focus. Cowell had both those qualities in spades. Speaking on the *This is Your Life* episode devoted to Cowell, music producer Pete Waterman recalled of the young Cowell, 'His determination was phenomenal.' Having taught his son from an early age the importance of tenacity when chasing your dreams, Eric had injected fuel into the engine that drove Cowell's ambition.

It was another relative who first steered Cowell through the gates of the entertainment industry. His cousin Malcolm Christopher worked at Elstree Studios and gave Cowell a three-month position there as a runner. It's the classic entry job for the film and television industry, and is a lowly role that involves helping everything run smoothly and doing all the tasks nobody else wants to do. In a high-pressure environment, much of this involves running, hence the name. It isn't a glamorous role and Cowell worked 14-hour days for just £15 a week, doing such menial tasks as buying haemorrhoid cream for one of the high-up producers. He received no thanks for the ignominious transaction, quite the opposite actually, since the same piles-suffering producer decided Cowell couldn't stay on beyond his three-month trial. In the end he did stay, in defiance of the producer's orders, but he was quickly spotted and told to leave.

Cowell thought he would secure a speedy bounce-back from this rejection when he received word that legendary filmmaker Stanley Kubrick was embarking on a new film at Elstree. He applied for a job as a runner and was taken on. However, just two days into his new role, Cowell was told that Kubrick didn't want any runners on the project after all, so he went home and the legendary film *The Shining* was made without his assistance. However, Kubrick – who had just shaken hands on a deal to buy Abbots Mead, the Cowell family home – re-offered him a runners' job after having his ear bent by Eric as they toasted the property deal over several glasses of Scotch. By this time Cowell had received what he considered a much a better offer, and was ready to leave behind his dreams of working in the movies for a job in another sector of the entertainment industry.

# CHAPTER TWO

# 'OH, STROKE ME, DARLING!'

D on't let anyone tell you that the music industry is all about glamour. There was precious little of that around when Cowell rushed across busy central London roads with a bulging, wobbly mail trolley. His place of work wasn't exactly the height of chic either. He wasn't allowed to use the main entrance of the building, and the room in which he worked was cramped and had bars across the windows. His two closest colleagues were men of advanced years, one of whom had a bad case of the shakes. He got used to having unpleasant remarks hurled his way during the day. He could have been forgiven for thinking he was working in a prison and not for one of the biggest record labels in the world – and yet he couldn't have been happier.

So how did he find himself there and why was he so content? As his three-month trial at Elstree Studios was drawing to its conclusion, Cowell's parents had been secretly trying to secure him a job at the record label giant EMI. Eric was in charge of EMI's property wing, so the Cowell name had a certain amount of clout in the label's offices. Formed in March 1931, EMI has had such musical royalty as Judy Garland, Frank Sinatra, The Beatles, Beastie Boys and Radiohead signed to it, so any job there carried enormous excitement and potential for a youngster such as Cowell. Julie had written to EMI enquiring if there were any vacancies for her ambitious son, and within weeks her efforts came good and he was knocking on the door of the EMI personnel office, ready for an interview for a vacancy in the post room.

It was to be a lengthy interview – an hour and a half in total. Once more Cowell wore jeans, but this time he hit it off with his interviewer, Peter Schmidt. It's a name worth reporting because he's responsible for offering Cowell his first break in the music business, an industry he went on to generate hundreds of millions of pounds for. However, Cowell also had an offer from Kubrick. From dreaming about a job in entertainment, he now had two offers on the table. Cowell mulled over his options and decided to go for the job in the music industry, which is how he found himself working in the cramped mail room of EMI, surrounded by suspicions that he was little more than the beneficiary of nepotism, due to his father's connections with the company.

It might seem strange, then, that he was so happy with his lot. This was because he quickly identified a major benefit of working in the post room: he had access to all departments. Cowell was pushy and thought nothing of approaching the great and the good at EMI and asking for a promotion. He had only ever wanted a foot in the door; he was confident that once he was there he could quickly push his way into a better role. However, after eighteen months he realized that his undoubted chutzpah wasn't going to do the trick fast enough. After unsuccessfully trying to move to another label, he decided the music industry wasn't as great a career prospect as he had hoped. Cowell had had it with music and he asked his father to find him a job in the property industry, where his brother Nicholas was already making great strides. Eric quickly found Simon a job, but I'm sure you won't be surprised to learn that he quickly learned to hate life working as a junior in the estate agency world. He was given menial tasks and his personality clashed with his manager. It was at this point that Cowell sank to his lowest ebb, and yet again, his father came to the rescue by sorting out a return to EMI for his desperate son.

This time it was in a new department, where his task was to trawl through songs on the American EMI catalogue and attempt to place them with British artists. It was a small team and Cowell again faced an icy reception from his colleagues, who sniffed an air of nepotism in his appointment. However, he didn't buckle under the hostility, but instead got his head down and worked through the many thousands of songs in the American catalogue. This included many genres and it took a man with enormous patience to listen to each one in turn, while remaining focused enough to think which UK singers and bands might be good fits for each song. For nearly half a year he sat there becoming an unrivalled authority on the EMI international catalogue. It was a meticulous task requiring complete attention, and his painstaking work paid off.

Cowell had to learn on the job at this point and he learned fast. When he hit the road and met up with A&R men from other labels, he soon struck gold; within weeks he had nearly twenty songs tied-up with artists from other labels. It was the first moment that Cowell proved, not least to himself, that he could make it in the music business. His painstaking search of EMI's international catalogue had been married with an ability to correctly guess which domestic artists might work with each song. If he could pull that trick out of the bag, then surely he must have a good chance of being able to perform other more sexy music industry tricks, like knowing a hit when he heard it and successfully managing his own artists.

Meanwhile, Cowell was beginning to feel bored and stifled by the EMI environment. Not one to be frightened of risk, Cowell decided to take the audacious move of leaving EMI, going it alone and starting his own music business. It was a courageous decision. Many would have killed to have such a promising position at such a prestigious label, yet here was Cowell, throwing it away to go it alone at a very early point in his career. His gamble was not to be a success.

Cowell had been approached for this venture by his line manager at EMI, a man called Ellis Rich. Rich had been in the industry since 1963, starting out as an arranger. He also created transcriptions of rock songs, including those of Queen, and songbooks for buskers. A short, stocky man with extravagant white hair, he has always had a healthy amount of charm and charisma, so imagine how flattered Cowell must have been when Rich chose him to co-run his new business venture. The youngster had doubts, but he duly handed in his notice at EMI and the pair formed E&S Music. Their offices were in Soho, and Cowell quickly realized that he had made a huge mistake. Problems with funding, combined with an ignorance of a lot of what was required to run their own company meant that the writing was on the wall pretty quickly in

Cowell's eyes. Within weeks of leaving EMI he returned, begging to be let back. The response was a firm 'no'.

It isn't surprising that EMI shut the door in his face this time. It would have been his second 'return' within the space of a year. It was inconceivable that a huge company like EMI would allow a youngster to keep leaving and returning, so it was back to E&S for Cowell, where he did his best to make the venture work. The two partners flew to America and had a series of meetings in Los Angeles. They led to nothing in the end, but Cowell's head had been turned. He loved Los Angeles and seeing it for the first time fired his ambition once more. He loved the fun, glamour and warmth of the city, breathing it all in. Eventually, though, his early doubts about E&S's viability were confirmed. Continued problems with funding meant that Cowell threw in the towel just over a year after the company's formation and he and Rich went their separate ways. Since then, Rich has had noted chart success with his companies Supreme Songs and Independent Music Group and Cowell, well, he hasn't done so badly either.

Back then, though, it would have been understandable if Cowell had lost patience with the music industry altogether. Young people are often impatient for success and give up on a career path if it isn't quick to reap rewards. The world is littered with regretful people who gave up on their dreams in favour of a safer career path, and Cowell could easily have joined them. He had tried to make it via several routes, but hadn't managed to get as far as he would have liked. However, he wasn't about to give up. Instead, he simply reviewed and refined where he wanted to be in the industry and his key talent, which was, he believed, his ability to know on an almost instinctive level what it took to put together a hit single: a great asset in such an industry.

Cowell first connected with this instinct during those long months searching through the EMI international catalogue. When he managed to place many of the songs contained in the catalogue, he proved he had what it took to become an effective, one-man jukebox jury. The only problem was how to get a record label to share his confidence and give him a break. Enter Iain Burton.

Burton was a former dancer who had managed and guided the career of dancer and choreographer Arlene Phillips, who went on to become a reality show judge herself, on BBC1's *Strictly Come Dancing*. Cowell and Burton had got to know each other when Burton used to visit the EMI offices with his acts. As Cowell licked his wounds after leaving E&S, word reached him on the industry grapevine that Burton was looking to take some of the riches he had made from his management firm and start his own record label. Cowell quickly sensed an opportunity and the pair met up. Cowell's ambition and determination impressed Burton and they decided to give it a go, launching their own record label, Fanfare Records, which would finally propel Cowell to where he wanted to be.

Initially Fanfare Records' offices were in Burton's offices in the West End of London. Based on fashionable South Molton Street, it was a place that made the twenty-six-year-old Cowell – who was on a salary of £65 a week – feel thoroughly at home. There, just yards from Oxford Street and Bond Street, were trendy, glamorous women wherever his darting eyes looked and the whole area felt hip and happening. The first success of Fanfare Records came with the sale of a home fitness video featuring choreographer and dancer Arlene Phillips. Fitness videos were doing a healthy business overseas, but this was the first video of its genre made and sold in the UK, and it sold nearly half a million copies, injecting some much-needed capital into the fledgling venture. Cowell was pleased with this success and benefited from it, but ever hungry and ambitious, he was keen for his first big hit under the Fanfare umbrella. Before that happened, though, he was to meet two women who were to play an important role in his life.

One night he was drinking in a central London bar with a friend when an attractive woman walked in. He had been trying to charm a woman sitting at the next table but, in fickle male style, quickly transferred his attentions to the new arrival. Not only was he very attracted to her, she seemed strangely familiar. Her name was Jackie St Claire, and though he didn't realize it for a few days, he recognized her because she was the winner of the glamour competition Miss Nude UK.

The pair hit it off immediately, with St Claire finding Cowell the wittiest person she had ever met. He might have made her laugh, but inside he was extremely nervous in the presence of such a beautiful woman. Nerves would later threaten to ruin another important romantic relationship in Cowell's life.

Through Eric's membership of a posh Mayfair club, Cowell managed to impress St Claire on dates. She seemed to know how to play him, though, and would offer and then withdraw affection to keep him on his toes. After three months of this, the pair eventually decided just to be friends, an arrangement that has lasted to this day. Soon after he met her, Cowell encountered another attractive young woman with whom his personal relationship would follow a similar course, although they would also enjoy an important professional relationship.

Born in Seattle as one of twins, Sinitta Malone inherited her love of music from her mother, the soul/disco singer Miquel Brown, who had hits with songs such as 'So Many Men, So Little Time'. In her teens, Sinitta moved to England and attended a Bournemouth boarding school, while her mother toured the world with her successful singing career. Sinitta was fifteen when she first met Cowell – in a nightclub, he claims – and she quickly developed a crush on him. She would often have dinner with the Cowell family and was impressed by Julie's glamour and the hold she had over her sons, who were clearly devoted to her. They would compete for their mother's attention. Sometimes Julie would dismiss them and have girly chats with Sinitta, teaching her how to wax her legs and the like. At sixteen, Sinitta signed a record deal with Fanfare Records, and neither her nor Cowell's life would ever be the same again.

Cowell was impressed by Sinitta's voice when she played him her demo tapes. She seemed to have the whole package: she was beautiful and could dance too. No wonder he snapped her up for Fanfare Records. However, as Cowell has always maintained, it's the songs that create musical success, so he went to work finding a suitable track with which to give Sinitta her big break. A blast from his recent past soon sorted this out. During his days in the EMI post room, Cowell got to know a British songwriter called George Hargreaves. Recalling the young Cowell in a *Daily Mail* feature, Hargreaves wrote, 'He always had the air of someone who was going to be successful, and I wasn't at all surprised by how quickly he moved up from the post room to become a partner in a new record company called Fanfare Records.' It was there that their paths crossed once more. Hargreaves brought in a song he had written called 'So Macho'. In *I Don't Mean to Be Rude, But...*, Cowell says that as soon as he heard the song he was convinced it would be a hit. Hargreaves, however, claims that Cowell had major doubts about its commercial potential and needed heavy persuasion to release it.

Whether it was an instant decision or not, Cowell *did* decide that Sinitta could have a hit with 'So Macho'. Just as he was getting excited at the prospect, however, he had the wind taken out of his sails by a phone call from his partner Burton. Cowell was told by Burton that he had plans for a new direction and would consequently be closing down the music division of his new company. Just as Cowell was about to reach out and grasp his first big success, it seemed like it was going to be snatched away. However, we are talking about Simon Cowell, and he was never going to take Burton's news lying down. Instead, using his vast reserves of charm, influence and determination, he persuaded Burton to keep Fanfare Records going long enough for him to prove – via Sinitta and 'So Macho' – that he could make it work. He succeeded and was given a £5,000 budget to make 'So Macho' a hit. The pressure was well and truly on – could he do it?

Yes, he could. Working on a shoestring budget, and with Burton's axe ever closer to his neck, he managed to turn 'So Macho' into a handsome hit. True, it took three releases of the single before it took off, but when it did take off, it went all the way to number two at the end of 1985, selling 1.5 million copies.

From his £5,000 budget, the song produced a £1 million return. He had his first hit song and he was on his way. Convinced that Sinitta would be more than a one-hit wonder, the hunt was now on for a follow-up song. Turning 'So Macho' into a hit had taught him a lot about the process of hit-making, but as he searched for a suitable second single, he had to learn even more – and fast. One man in particular would do much of the teaching. He was to become a profound influence in Cowell's career.

Pete Waterman was born in Coventry in January 1947. The city was in ruins after the Second World War and his family was poor. Electricity would only be turned on in their household in the evening, when his father returned home from work. Waterman left school semi-literate and with few qualifications. He then took a series of jobs, including working as a gravedigger, on the railways, as a coal miner and then a nightclub disc jockey. In their different ways, all four were to make him a tough and determined man. After seeing The Beatles live, he was determined to move into music, and eventually formed the Stock Aitken Waterman partnership with songwriters and producers Mike Stock and Matt Aitken. It quickly became a hit factory.

Cowell heard of Stock Aitken Waterman early in their career and believed that they were a team that could deliver Sinitta's second hit. However, Waterman was a brusque man with extraordinary reserves of self-confidence. Cowell was hardly a shrinking violet himself, but he'd met his match in the Coventry-born producer. When the pair met at Waterman's chaotic recording studio, Cowell found that despite his persistence, the producer wasn't willing at this point to work with Sinitta. Knowing he was on the crest of a wave, Waterman wasn't prepared to be distracted. Soon after this meeting he became a major player in the industry, dominating the pop charts. Cowell was not to give up on his quest to work with Waterman, though. Indeed, he has since said that that initially unsuccessful meeting was the most important day of his career.

Meanwhile, Sinitta was doing her best to maintain the profile she had built up with 'So Macho', performing in nightclubs and making appearances across the country. However, there's only so long an artist can play off one hit before another is needed to keep them in the public eye, and Cowell was determined that Waterman would be the man to produce that hit. In his own words, Cowell more or less stalked the producer, watching how he and the industry worked. Every time Waterman turned round, Cowell would be watching him.

One day he asked the youngster what he wanted. To learn from you, replied Cowell. 'I'm not going to pay you,' warned a sceptical Waterman. Cowell didn't care about being paid at this point, though, since he considered the crash-course he was receiving to be far more valuable than a salary. As he learned from Waterman, he would also continue to beg him to write and produce a single for Sinitta. He would be told no, often in very impolite terms. Waterman has never been a man to mince his words. Decades later, speaking on the second of two episodes of *This is Your Life* that were devoted to Cowell's career, he put into context how important these times with Waterman were to his own professional development. 'I knew instinctively he was a genius,' Cowell told Sir Trevor McDonald. 'I had no money, I had one artist. I followed him around for two years and he taught me the fundamentals of the business. He was very generous to give me his time. I always said, the person who put me on the right path was Pete Waterman. Still to this day if I need advice, the person I will go to is Pete Waterman. He's a good guy.' Waterman was moved by Cowell's words on the show and their mutual respect was palpable on the night.

Back in the 1980s, as Cowell tried to persuade Waterman to work with Sinitta, he realized it was just a matter of finding the right song. This was easier said than done, even for a rising star like Cowell. Then, one day, says Cowell, he read a newspaper feature about how female celebrities were beginning to date increasingly younger men, or toyboys as they were known. Something clicked in Cowell's head and he picked up the phone and rang Waterman, who finally agreed to work with him, bringing to an end the 'dog' years, as Cowell has described them.

As he put it: 'It took me about two years to eventually persuade him to work for me. And within that two-year period, I followed him around like a dog because I knew that this guy could teach me more in a year or two than I could learn in twenty-five years within a major corporation.' The benefits of this unconventional education were about to pay off.

The genesis of the song 'Toyboy' is in some dispute. Cowell claims the credit for it via his newspaper-feature inspiration, but Mike Stock claims the inspiration came from Sinitta herself. One way or another, though, Sinitta's second hit, 'Toyboy', was born. Written and produced by Waterman, it's a glorious romp of a pop song in which Sinitta sings with joy of her little boy plaything. Good fun, great lyrics and a catchy tune, it was pop gold. Quite literally in fact, as it went on to sell millions of copies in countries across the world. It reached number four in the British charts in July 1987, and remained in the charts for a laudable fourteen weeks. Sinitta was getting comfortable in the Top Forty, which was a good job, as she quickly had five more hit singles, including 'I Don't Believe In Miracles' (released in 1988) and 'Love On A Mountaintop' (released in 1989). Her fame was international and she did particularly well in the Japanese market.

It was during this time that Cowell became close to Sinitta personally, though there is some confusion as to how close they were. In his book, Cowell says that they dated during this period, but Sinitta has denied that they ever made love. As she told the *Daily Mail*, he would be quite open about this in public. 'We'd be out to dinner and he'd say, "Sinitta and sex, for me it doesn't happen,"' she said, adding that this sort of behaviour would leave her 'endlessly embarrassed and upset'. They did share a bed on occasion, but according to her, what went on there barely consisted of foreplay. 'He loved being stroked and petted on his head. "Oh, stroke me, darling," he'd say.' Whatever the case, their relationship was one that meant a great deal to her as she rated Cowell as the only constant male presence in her life and like a combination of father, brother and boyfriend. 'Once I became well known, he was an anchor,' she says. She was close to his parents too, both of whom were extremely fond of her and very protective. She became almost a surrogate daughter and must have drawn enormous joy from being an unofficial part of such a warm and loving family unit. At one point they formally became her guardians, because in order to travel overseas to work at sixteen, she required official chaperones. Ever a warm and kind couple, Eric and Julie were more than happy to oblige.

Eventually, Cowell and Sinitta dropped any romantic side of their relationship that might have existed and kept things purely professional. Their relationship remains strong to this day on both a friendship level and also – of late – on a professional one, since she has been a key figure in the success of *The X Factor*. They have been good for one another in so many ways. Cowell brought her a family unit and a strong male figure, both of which she needed at a young age, while Sinitta gave Cowell his first hit, enabling him to get the attention of Pete Waterman, who has guided his career and who remains a close friend and contact to this day. Cowell and Sinitta are a tight pair. As *X Factor* contestant Niki Evans said, 'She knows him inside and out. You wouldn't want to cross Simon because she'd rip your head off and shit down your neck for him. She loves him and he loves her. They've got so much mutual respect for each other.'

At the time, Cowell struck an impressive figure to the outside world. He owned his own record label, drove a convertible Porsche, had a house in Fulham and partied most nights. He was, in his own words, a 1980s stereotype. 'In the Eighties I had my own record business,' he said. 'I was a typical Eighties cliché. I had the cars, the house, the image, and everything was beyond my means. I spent too much time at parties and then everything imploded.' Intoxicated by the atmosphere of the 1980s yuppie culture, he invested heavily in shares and, as he told *Playboy* magazine, 'Basically... they crashed.' Suddenly Cowell realized he had no money left. Indeed, it was far worse than that: he owed nearly half a million pounds to the bank. 'I realized I had to give everything back – the Porsche, the big house – and I wasn't crying,' he said.

He claims to have found the experience something of a relief, and says it was the best thing that could have happened to him. Cowell had to move back to his parents' home, not an easy move for a man in his early thirties. He got a taxi there and realized that the four pounds he used to pay the fare was the last bit of money he had in the world. (One wonders why, if he was so short of cash, he didn't take the cheaper option of public transport. Perhaps he had a lot of luggage?) He insists he wasn't at all embarrassed about moving back in with his parents. 'Not in the slightest,' he told *The Observer*. 'I didn't lie to anyone about it and I certainly wasn't treated any differently by my friends or family. It was almost a sense of release in a strange way, like all these burdens suddenly disappeared, and I genuinely didn't miss any of them. I bought an old TR6, and I loved that car more than the Porsche. Obviously I didn't take flash holidays, and I lived on maybe £150–200 a week, but I managed fine. I can't say I was any more unhappy then than I am now. I've always been fairly jittery, you know. I've never believed this is going to last for ever.'

This is quintessential Cowell: the ability to find the positive in a setback, not just in retrospect as a happy-clappy media spin, but to genuinely look on the bright side and turn the situation to his advantage. This period in his life was a significant wake-up call for him. 'It came on the back of a very artificial time in Britain, where everyone was buying things they couldn't afford, and it was always going to blow up in our faces,' he says. He was confronted with the horrible truth about himself: the Porsche, the house in Fulham, none of it was really his. 'The real story was that I didn't actually own the things I had. I had a mortgage for the house, loans for the car – nothing was real.' He made a vow there and then that he would never borrow again. Anything he wanted from now on, he would only get when he could afford to buy it outright.

He had lost so much, but the one thing he held on to was his determination. 'There was a weird sense of freedom at having absolutely zilch, but still having the energy and desire to change my life for the better,' he says. 'Losing everything is probably the greatest lesson you learn. I went back to my parents' house and started again. From then on everything I did was different. It was all about the work.' There were other more immediate advantages, too, such as enjoying his parents' cooking while he planned how to rebuild his career. Cowell enjoyed this period because he's always believed that getting to the top is more fun than being there.

Despite the relentless positivity about this time of his life, and his insistence that he isn't ashamed of it, it should be noted that he doesn't mention moving back to his parents' house in the first edition of his book, *I Don't Mean to Be Rude, But...* Instead, he glosses over the entire period. The book's narrative moves from 1985 (when he and Burton parted company) and 1989 (when he joined BMG and began his second coming) in three paragraphs, without mentioning his financial disaster. He spent several years back at his parents'. 'I was quite happy, really,' he says now. 'I looked at it as a new start, and this time, I wanted my own company.' He was ready to bounce back from this setback, but no one could have predicted quite how spectacularly he would do so.

Perhaps some employees of the label BMG had an inkling of what Cowell was capable of. A big player in the record label sphere, BMG was founded in 1987. It had been covering the distribution side of Fanfare Records for some months when, in 1989, it contacted Cowell to offer him a job as an A&R consultant. Despite the disdain he'd built up for the A&R community during his days at EMI, Cowell jumped at the chance. The position offered him the ideal combination of security and freedom. His job was simply to grab hot new artists, even hotter new songs and weld them into a package that would shift – to use record industry parlance – as many units as possible. It was a job that required tireless determination and a knack for what constituted a hit.

Cowell could certainly manage that.

# CHAPTER THREE

# 'It's about Dad...'

D uring the 1980s, television became dramatically more influential on other areas of the media. For instance, the success of the *Sun* newspaper during the decade was due in part to the fact that it recognized and submitted to the extraordinary power of television, which rose even higher with the launch of satellite TV. Stories about television personalities, shows and soap operas became a key part of its content. As well as its daily television listings, it devoted whole pages to television critics and gossip, and regularly splashed stories about *Coronation Street* and *EastEnders* on its front page. The *Sun* – and other similar tabloid newspapers – didn't sit and wring its hands about the influence of 'trashy television', nor did it mourn how much of its influence and power television had taken. Instead, it simply moved with the times and cleaned up off the back of TV's influential rise.

It wasn't just tabloid editors who had this vision, though, Simon Cowell did too. Indeed, he felt that television was about to have an even bigger influence on the music industry than it had elsewhere. Satellite music channels ensured that artists spent a fortune getting their promotional videos perfect, as the small screen superseded the radio as the place to make or break a record. This, Cowell believed, was only the beginning of how the audio and visual mediums could coincide profitably. He would not have claimed to be the biggest 'muso' expert, but he could spot a trend a mile off, and the next big thing in the music industry was going to involve TV show tie-ins. Gone were the days when the only way to break a new pop act was via the tried, tested (and tiresome) radio plugging route. His message was not an apocalyptic adapt-or-die one, though. Cowell was too busy working out how much money he could make from selling records with a television tie-in. His calculation: lots and lots and lots.

Like many entrepreneurially minded people, he faced a great deal of resistance. It wasn't just a lack of vision among his colleagues, it was a snobbery against his mass-market approach. 'You know, it's a funny thing about the music industry which is quite unusual,' he told the *Fresh Air* radio show. 'I think in television and film, it's readily accepted that both TV and film has to survive as an industry by selling to all sorts of demographics. I mean, you have children's TV. You have more serious TV. You have mass-market TV. My theory about the music industry is, why shouldn't we run the record label with that concept, which is, of course, you can have the more credible serious stuff, but why shouldn't a younger audience be able to buy music they like, which isn't necessarily the most artistic form on Earth, but they love when they buy it? I mean, I've never seen the sense of being snobbish about music. You either like it or you don't.'

Credibility has never been a word Cowell has been overly concerned with, certainly not when compared with his interest in words like 'profit' and 'success'. He was about to have plenty of the latter with the next two acts he promoted. Both were already enormously successful on television, but it was Cowell who first spotted their potential to sell millions of records. In the second half of the 1980s, the World Wrestling Federation (WWF) hit something of a golden era, and Cowell had a eureka moment one day about how he could get a slice of that success. 'I read in one of our newspapers that they'd sold out eighty-two thousand seats in twenty-seven minutes. Hang on a minute, there's not a rock band in the world [that] can do that. And I also found out that they were selling about two and a half million videos a year to the fans who watch the show. So it didn't take a lot of time to realize that if they were selling that many seats and that many videos, there would be a lot of kids who would want to buy an album from the wrestlers as well. It was just common sense.' Full of excitement and urgency, he contacted the bosses of WWF and managed to get a meeting with them. His legendary charm and belief won them over, and they quickly signed up to release a WWF record through the BMG label he was then representing, Arista Records.

The result was 'Slam Jam', written and produced by Pete Waterman and Mike Stock. It was a glorious cheesy effort that included quotes from WWF fighters, including Brett 'Hit Man' Hart and 'Macho Man' Randy Savage. With loud, colourful packaging and a wonderful video to back it, 'Slam Jam' went straight to number four and spent nine weeks in the Top Forty. The album that followed soon after sold 1.5 million copies in Europe. Cowell had answered the scepticism of detractors with sheer commercial figures. One of those detractors had, memorably, sunk to his knees and begged Cowell not to go ahead with the WWF deal. Cowell resented the lack of support and enthusiasm from his colleagues for his venture, but one can't help but think he'd have enjoyed the sight of a senior executive on his knees begging him about anything.

The WWF era of Cowell's career has become something that's regularly commented upon, often disparagingly. For instance, as *Pop Idol* fever swept Britain in the winter of 2001, the *Sun* turned the tables on the newly infamous Cowell by delivering its own withering verdict on songs from his back catalogue. Of 'Slam Jam', the article said, 'This song has a lot to answer for. Its success helped to convince Simon there was money to be made out of novelty records. And let's face it, nobody was going to tell wrestlers they couldn't sing.'

Nobody was going to tell Cowell that there was anything less than oodles of cash to be made from the television industry, either. He was itching for his next big deal, and he had only to switch on his television one morning to enjoy his next eureka moment. Having had enormous success with a gang of wrestlers, he was set to cash in on the success of a couple of breakfast television puppets. Zig & Zag were first seen on Irish TV's RTE 2 in a children's show called *Dempsey's Den*. They then came to prominence in the UK via the madcap Channel 4 breakfast television show *The Big Breakfast*, which launched in September 1992. They had their own slot on the show called 'The Crunch', followed by cameo roles during the rest of the day's broadcast, and they enjoyed banter with the presenters, Chris Evans and Gaby Roslin. The British public quickly fell in love with the puppets and couldn't get enough of their early-morning antics. Fresh from his WWF success, Cowell soon had a plan for another nice little earner.

There was already a precedent of a breakfast-television puppet having a hit single in Britain. In the early 1980s, Roland Rat first appeared on our television screens on ITV's breakfast show *TV-am*. The show was struggling at that point in its history, and the rodent puppet is often credited with saving it. As producer Greg Dyke quipped, Roland was 'the first rat to join a sinking ship'. With the puppet onboard, *TV-am* sailed into calmer waters as viewers of all ages fell in love with the cheeky rascal and his friends, including Kevin the Gerbil. In 1983, the first Roland Rat single was released. 'Rat Rapping' was a smash-hit song that was followed by two further singles. An album was then released, which included tracks produced by Stock Aitken Waterman. However, this fared less well and the musical career of Roland Rat was soon over. Still, how many rodents can say they saved a television show from cancellation?

The success of the Roland Rat singles was enough to show that popular television puppets could have commercially successful music careers. In the early 1990s Zig & Zag followed the example of Roland Rat and released three singles, 'Zig Zaggin' Around', 'Them Girls' and 'Hands Up', plus a subsequent album. Cowell was the mastermind behind these successes and today, he says of the Zig & Zag era, 'It wasn't my proudest moment, but it was a hit.' Yet again, he had faced opposition from his colleagues. When he announced to a board meeting that he was planning to release songs with the puppets, he noticed some barely suppressed giggling. A director insisted that Cowell play them the demo of the song, and when he did, the director drew an enormous 'zero' on a piece of paper. Cowell walked out and moved to another label, RCA. Founded in 1901, the label's initials stand for Radio

Corporation of America, and it became part of the BMG group in the mid-1990s. At RCA, he found a more supportive atmosphere and quickly made friends with two of the management. Here, Cowell felt far more at home. RCA released the Zig & Zag records and reaped the rewards.

Speaking of puppets, rumours suggest that in the early 1980s, Cowell himself dressed up in a furry outfit in order to promote a single on television. The single in question was called 'Ruff Mix', in which sampled sounds of dogs barking were played over a pop tune. The song was catchy and cheesy – it was released in 1982 – and despite some horrendous reviews – 'This has to be the worst record of all time. It's a real stinker,' said one critic – the single reached number 31 in the charts. How far Cowell's involvement in the song went is a matter of debate. The man himself says only that he was 'involved' in making the song, but others insist that his voice can be heard barking on the song and that he dressed up in a dog outfit to promote the single on television. The following year, the same act, called Wonder Dog, returned with a Christmas single called 'Christmas Tail'.

Whatever the extent of his involvement in Wonder Dog, Cowell definitely put out some material recorded by the characters of action television show *Power Rangers*. He had noted their enormous success both in television viewing figures and in the sales of toys and related merchandise. Why, he thought, should there not be musical merchandise, too? Quickly he signed the deal to release *Power Rangers* songs and the singles went into the top three (as had the Zig & Zag releases). The two acts eventually sold 1.5 million records between them. Let the snobs giggle and sneer all they liked, Cowell was laughing all the way to the bank.

However, he also believed that he had only begun to scratch the surface of what was possible when you combined the music and television industries. His ambition and fierce competitiveness was ready to propel him on to even greater heights.

His next big act had a television angle of sorts, but was closer to the Sinitta model than the Power Rangers one. Born Sonia Evans in 1971, the cheeky Liverpudlian redhead became better known simply as Sonia when her musical career was launched in 1989 by Stock Aitken Waterman. Her method of getting Waterman's attention was not dissimilar to Cowell's in that she turned up outside his recording studio one day and asked him to listen to her sing. He was impressed and quickly turned her into a hit pop act with five Top Twenty hits. She recorded 'You've Got A Friend' (a favourite song of Cowell's incidentally) as a charity single for ChildLine and sang on Band Aid II's 1989 reprise of 'Do They Know It's Christmas?'. As her fame grew, she came second in the Eurovision Song Contest with her cover of 'Better The Devil You Know'. Cowell had been tracking her success and signed her to BMG in 1992, releasing her Eurovision song and other singles, including 'Boogie Nights'. In his book he describes her with one word: 'sweet'. Sweet Sonia's young backing dancers soon formed a band called Chaos; the five-piece were signed by Cowell and renamed Ultimate Kaos and soon they were having chart success of their own.

Another act signed by Cowell at this time was a pop act called Curiosity, though most readers will remember them better as Curiosity Killed the Cat. Signed to Mercury Records, they had chart success in the 1980s with songs such as 'Down To Earth', 'Misfit' and 'First Place'. Their first album went to number one, but their second was less successful, leading them to be dropped by Mercury. By now they were called just Curiosity and were signed to RCA by Cowell. There they returned to the Top Ten with their first single with their new label, but they soon returned to obscurity. Cowell says he found them 'difficult' to work with, but he can be proud that he took a falling band and put them back in the Top Ten. Just as he found Curiosity difficult to work with, so he would find the next act he worked with easy – and very, very profitable. And once again, he would find them not at a pop audition, but on his television screen.

*Soldier, Soldier* was produced by Central Television and first broadcast on ITV in 1991. It was a massively popular drama that focused on a fictional British army infantry unit. These were interesting times for the British military: the Cold War had just ended and the Allies had enjoyed a relatively easy victory in the first Gulf War, which had been sparked by Iraqi dictator Saddam Hussein's invasion of Kuwait. In the real world, however, the army was being downsized, and this was reflected on-screen in *Soldier, Soldier*. It wasn't an overly gritty programme – it was a time of peace and therefore the drama was more of the everyday than combative variety.

Perhaps the most popular characters on the show, which ran for seven series, were played by Robson Green and Jerome Flynn, who appeared as Fusilier Dave Tucker and Lance Corporal Paddy Garvey respectively. During one episode, broadcast in 1995, the duo sang the Righteous Brothers' 'Unchained Melody'. It's one of the most recorded songs of the twentieth century as well as being a soul classic and a favourite of many music lovers, including one

Simon Cowell. His love of the song was about to take on a whole new dimension, though, as he went on to have a runaway hit with Robson and Jerome's version. However, getting that hit was going to require even more determination and perseverance than he had ever shown before. Huge obstacles would be put in his path, but he went on to overcome them all and reach the finishing line in style.

In the wake of the *Soldier, Soldier* episode in which 'Unchained Melody' was performed, the public went mad for the song. Viewers had so enjoyed it that they phoned record stores and record labels asking where they could get their hands on Robson and Jerome's version. The nation was going 'Unchained Melody' barmy. Among those who were swept up in the madness were Cowell's brother Nicholas and a colleague from RCA. Both brought the craze to Cowell's attention, knowing how good he was at turning television hits into hit songs. Cowell listened to what they had to say and put in a few calls to investigate just how much interest there was. He quickly sniffed the potential for a major hit and excitedly picked up the phone to tell the two actors about the money-making prospect he had in store for them.

However, when he attempted to put the idea to Robson Green and Jerome Flynn, he hit a brick wall: the pair seemed totally uninterested. He tried every way possible to change their minds, bombarding them with messages via post, phone, fax and even written pleas delivered by hand. He was, by his own admission, harassing them, such was his belief in the potential they had as recording artists, off the back of the popularity of *Soldier, Soldier*. So persistent was his campaign that Cowell even received a warning of legal action from Robson Green if he didn't leave them alone.

Around this time Cowell took a holiday abroad, but still he couldn't stop thinking about 'Unchained Melody' and its commercial potential – so much so that he ended up flying home early and continuing to pursue the two actors. On one day alone the number of calls he made to them ran into double figures. 'He stalked me and harassed my mother for two months,' said Robson on *This is Your Life*.

'It's true,' said Cowell. 'I went on holiday and thought, "Oh sod it, I'll start on the mother."' Eventually, the pressure told and he received a furious phone call direct from Robson Green. Using all his formidable charm, Cowell managed to calm the actor down and arranged to meet with him to discuss the idea.

Once he finally had the two actors in front of him, Cowell soon got them to agree to record 'Unchained Melody', on the condition that they wouldn't be required to appear on *Top of the Pops* to promote or perform it. At last he had the deal he had dreamt of and tirelessly striven for. Would the single do as well as he hoped? There were doubts among some at the record label, but all those doubts evaporated when the single sailed straight to number one – and stayed there for seven weeks. Robson and Jerome had landed Cowell his longed-for number one and were about to make him his first million.

Cowell quickly focused on the follow-up single, which was a double-A-side featuring 'I Believe' and 'Up On The Roof'. He arranged for them to give their first performance of the single on the *National Lottery Show*, and the single became another number one, selling over a million copies in its first week.

It wasn't just the *National Lottery Show* they appeared on either. Inevitably the two actors relented and agreed to appear on *Top of the Pops*. ('I knew they would,' boasted Cowell in his autobiography.) It was a memorable night for them. They had to avoid crossing paths with Oasis, who were furious with the duo for keeping their single 'Wonderwall' off the number-one spot. Then, while they were singing, Robson noticed someone in the studio audience wearing a T-shirt with an interesting slogan written on it: 'Robson and Jerome are a load of old bollocks'. Such sentiments were drowned out by the appreciation of most of the audience, though, and of the record-buying public. Cowell's unprecedented commitment and determination to bring Robson and Jerome to the music charts paid off in style. It's easy to imagine him basking not just in the profits, but in the associated glow of vindication too.

The media were beginning to take notice of Cowell, too. Who was this record executive with an eye for making hit records off the back of mass-market television shows? Articles on Cowell began appearing not just in the music trade press but in the national newspapers. One such story was topped by a headline that Cowell must have taken particular pride in: 'They're naff, they're corny and they're number one' ran the header in the *Evening Standard*. Their naffness had cost them the support of Radio 1, who refused to play Robson and Jerome's material and dubbed Cowell the antichrist of the music business. Radio 2, though, was a different matter. 'Their songs are so strong, they're obvious choices for our playlist,' said a spokesman.

But although the media were beginning to notice Cowell, some people in the music industry were less than enamoured with him. 'I would rather listen to Frank Bruno's [cover of] "Eye of the

Tiger" all day, every day for the rest of my life, than those *Soldier Soldier* boys,' said one unnamed promotions figure. 'People in the industry have no regard for them at all.' The record-buying public did, though, and once again Cowell was laughing all the way to the bank. He had become a millionaire, thanks to his extraordinary persistence. 'It took me four months to persuade the boys,' Cowell discloses. 'They just didn't see themselves as potential pop stars.' They were four months well spent.

Having released two singles, Robson and Jerome then put out two best-selling albums: *Robson & Jerome* and *Take Two*. Cowell selected the track lists for each album by assessing what songs were most popular in the UK's karaoke bars. A simple, democratic and genius way to ensure popularity or, to put it another way, he had the common touch. Cowell offered the actors three million pounds to record a third album, but at this point they chose to shake hands and return to their first love: acting. They had sold five million singles and seven million albums and enjoyed a hell of a ride. Cowell speaks very warmly of the pair, not just because of the money they made him, but for their decency and professionalism. He really enjoyed working with them.

It's a warmth that's reciprocated. Thanks to his association with Cowell, the advantages for Robson Green went beyond the financial and professional. Cowell introduced him to a colleague of his called Vanya Seager, a former model and Bond Girl in *For Your Eyes Only*. She had also done some topless modelling and was friends with Cowell before he employed her as his PA at RCA, which is where she met Green. Some years later, they got married and had a son called Taylor. 'It is no exaggeration to say', said

Green to the *Daily Mail*, 'that Vanya and I would never have got together had it not been for "Unchained Melody".' He joked in the same interview that this means he has plenty of dirt on Cowell, should he ever need to call on it.

As for Cowell, he told the *Daily Mail* about how he introduced the couple. 'She is very popular but very private,' said her boss. 'She never told me who her boyfriend was and I didn't know it was him until she had left. She was my secretary for years and years... but they were incredibly discreet about what was going on. She left in October and just said she had a new boyfriend she wanted to look after and spend more time with. I knew about the topless modelling when I employed her because we have been friends for a long time. We were friends before I gave her the job.' He seemed comfortable in the role of cupid, though it's probably not a role the public could imagine him being good at.

Green has plenty of reasons to be grateful to Cowell, but that hasn't stopped him being critical of some of Cowell's work. 'When I look at those... *Pop Idol* kids by comparison to Jerome and me, I can't help but think they're being fleeced.' Speaking to *The Daily Telegraph*, he added, 'He's superb at making money. That is his pursuit. That is what Simon Cowell is. But my instincts are very uncomfortable with what he does. I mean, we were OK because we were in our thirties when it happened and we had good solid careers. But the thing about *American Idol* and every other reality show is that it uses young people, who rightly or wrongly will do anything to be recognized, to seek approval. I mean, you're mentally scarring young kids... how do you recover from all that at that really, really vulnerable age? And the other thing with *Idol* and those sorts of things is the contestants are missing out on all the arts of the apprenticeship. They're saying, "You can get to the top right now, people will love you in their millions." But it will last a very short time and you will probably need therapy afterwards.' Despite this criticism, he has also spoken highly of Cowell and their time together, calling him 'one of the good guys' when he appeared on *This is Your Life*.

Cowell, meanwhile, continued with what he was good at: identifying which successful television programmes were ripe for musical exploitation and making sure he was the man who cashed in. In 1997, he spotted another chance. The Teletubbies were four brightly coloured characters that soon became popular through their BBC children's television series of the same name. Tinky Winky, Dipsy, Laa-Laa and Po were household favourites, enjoyed not just by the children they were aimed at, but by their parents and students, too. They communicated in garbled squeaky voices and had bizarre catchphrases such as, 'Eh oh, Laa-Laa.'

As their popularity soared during the first year on air, Cowell acted quickly. He heard a rumour that rival record label Sony were planning to sign up the *Teletubbies* for a novelty single. He had never even seen the show, but told the *Sun*, 'I got the BBC in my office and told them I would give them five hundred thousand in advance. We knew a record like that would make over two million.' The resulting record, 'Teletubbies Say Eh-Oh', was released in December 1997 and went straight to number one, where it remained for two weeks. Could it go on to grab the highly prized Christmas number-one slot, wondered Cowell. William Hill the bookmakers thought it could, making it their favourite for the slot at odds of 6:4. Siobhan Ennis, a manager at Tower

Records' Piccadilly Circus store showed that the retail industry was hopeful too. She told *The Times*, 'The race for the Christmas number one is really exciting. At this time of year, people aren't being so serious about their purchasing. We've taken a hell of a lot of the Teletubbies record. The singles market is driven by children, and not just at Christmas.' No wonder Cowell was in such bullish and optimistic mood. 'It will definitely be Christmas number one,' he told *Music Week* magazine.

However, this wasn't to be Cowell's first Christmas number one. The single sold well, remaining in the Top Seventy Five for twenty-nine weeks and even being nominated for an Ivor Novello Award in the British single category. However, it was beaten to the Christmas number one spot by The Spice Girls' ballad 'Too Much'.

The Spice Girls were a band with whom Cowell had a certain amount of history. His famously cool manner must have been a bit ruffled when he watched them conquer the world and sell fifty-five million records across the globe. Their nine number-one singles in the United Kingdom is equal to those enjoyed by Abba. Their ticket sales and merchandise revenue were staggering and they became one of the biggest pop bands of all time. And they had slipped through Cowell's fingers...

Originally called Touch, the band changed their name to Spice in 1993. It was soon after this that Cowell got word of a new British girl group who were being tipped for success and were searching for a record deal. He met them and they played him their proposed debut single, the song with which they planned to conquer the world. They were sitting in a van in London as they played Cowell the recording of a song called 'Wannabe'. He was, to use one of his favourite on-air phrases, blown away by the song and the girls, and he immediately rang their manager, promising to give him twice what any other label had offered for the band's signature. He was too late, though, for the band had just signed with Virgin Records – and the rest is history of the global sensation variety.

It's a history that also includes a second successive Cowell/Spice Girls head-to-head for the Christmas number one slot. Having come second to the girls in 1997 with his Teletubbies single, he found himself up against them again in 1998. This time his act was a seventeen-year-old north Londoner called Alberta Sheriff with a single called 'Yo Yo Boy'. Sherrif had been the runner-up in the Great British Song Contest, the BBC show that determined which song would represent the UK at Eurovision. Having seen his confidence dashed the previous year, this time Cowell was more blasé in his comments to *Music Week*. 'I've given up trying to have a Christmas number one. I've been the bridesmaid so many times now. If we're number two in December it will be fantastic,' he said. Once more he was pipped to the post by the Spice Girls. Cowell might have kicked himself for missing out on the girl-band sensation, but as we now know, he would go on to make a fortune working on another project with their manager. His name? Simon Fuller.

Nevertheless, to miss out on the Spice Girls must have been devastating for him – nearly as bad as turning down Take That, which in a way he did, after the band walked into his office one morning in the 1990s. They had some rough demos of their music and some photographs of them posing pop-star style. He claims he told them to 'sack the fat one' – by which he meant Gary Barlow – then he would sign them. 'He was overweight at the time with a weird haircut,' Cowell said on *This is Your Life*. Barlow has since disputed this story, saying that Cowell actually advised them to go to a different label. Either way, they weren't signed up to Cowell's label. 'I realized three months later that I'd made a mistake,' admitted Cowell in the *Mirror*. 'Everyone was talking about them. I went back and said I'd changed my mind, but it was too late. With every number one hit they had – and there were eight of them – I felt physically ill, but you have to hold your hands up and say, "I screwed up". I tend to go very quiet for a couple of weeks, then it's over. I just get on with it.'

In the wake of missing out on these two acts, Cowell was determined to 'just get on with it' in style by putting together his own all-conquering pop band. To this end, he turned to one of the men who formed the Spice Girls, Chris Herbert. Surrey-born Herbert was the original manager of the band and had therefore proved he could pick, form and mould a killer pop proposition. Advertisements were placed in *The Stage* in 1997, asking for young men who could sing and dance to audition for a new pop band 'with attitude and edge'. After auditioning 3,000 applicants, Herbert and a colleague narrowed down the field to just fourteen hopefuls. Soon they had a finished band that contained five members and would be called Five. They rehearsed at the same studio the Spice Girls had practised at. Indeed, they were like a male Spice Girls, a mixture of spiky, sexy individuals who had more life to them than traditional boy bands. Cowell was delighted with the result and signed the band to RCA on a six-album deal.

Their first hit was a catchy pop tune called 'Slam Dunk Da Funk', released in November 1997. It was an instant hit and soon Five were regulars in the charts, on television and in teen magazines. They sold ten million records across the globe, with eleven Top Ten singles and four Top Ten albums in the UK. Having watched in silent horror as Take That and the Spice Girls ripped up the charts, Cowell finally had his own multi-million-selling pop act. However, for this ultra-competitive man, the relief was only partial. 'It made me feel a little better,' he wrote of their success. But as he also reveals, he narrowly missed out on getting the rights to a song called 'Baby One More Time' for Five. However much he begged the songwriter to give Five the song, it went elsewhere and launched the pop career of a young lady from Louisiana, America. Her name? Britney Spears.

As Five's career neared its end, Cowell missed out on another band that went on to become sensationally successful. Busted were a three-piece pop act with a difference: they played their own guitars and wrote their own music. With the handsome Charlie Simpson, the wild Matt Willis and the cute, talented James Bourne, they were all set for success when they came to see Cowell, but he insisted they should introduce a full-time drummer to their line-up.

Bourne was, as he later told news website Ananova, fearful of how Cowell would manage them. 'It would have been a dictatorship,' he said. 'No matter what anyone says, Simon Cowell, he would tell you what to do.' In the end the band went with Universal Records and sold over three million records in the United Kingdom – without a full-time drummer.

Five split in 2001 and Busted parted company four years

later, but by then Cowell had a new boyband on his hands. They had a different image and sound to Five, and would go on to become a terrifyingly successful act, whose tally of UK number ones came behind only Elvis Presley and The Beatles. As the legend goes, one night in July 1998, Irish music impresario Louis Walsh noticed a three-piece boy band rehearsing in a car park in Dublin. The three boys going through their paces were called Shane Filan, Kian Egan and Mark Feehily. He linked them up with two other boys, Nicky Byrne and Brian McFadden, and suddenly he had an exciting pop prospect on his hands. Now he just needed a record deal. He phoned Cowell and ordered him to fly to the Emerald Isle and check out his new band, who were called IOU. Understandably, Cowell was less than impressed by the unevocative band name, but Walsh heaped on the pressure, saying they had the best voices he had ever witnessed and looked 'amazing, just amazing'.

Walsh was a man that people in the music industry listened to, thanks to his incredible track record. Born in County Mayo in 1955, Walsh was the second oldest of nine children. When he left school he moved to Ireland's capital, Dublin, and worked as an entertainment booker for twenty years. It was tough work, but it taught him how the industry operated. Walsh went on to enjoy massive success with Irish boyband Boyzone, who he put together in 1993. By 1999, they had already sold most of the approaching twenty million records they would ultimately shift, and the act he wanted to introduce to Cowell had, he believed, even greater potential. He just hoped that Cowell could see it, too.

Cowell has famously strong powers of persuasion, but so does Walsh, and the following morning Cowell was on a plane to Ireland to see the Irishman's new charges. He and Walsh were vaguely familiar with each other at this point. Working in the same industry, they had met, but had yet to work together on the same project. All this was about to change, though, and neither of their careers would ever be the same again.

Cowell was staying in a luxurious hotel in the Irish capital when Walsh knocked on the door of his suite with the five members of IOU in tow. When he clapped eyes on the band, Cowell's heart sank. He wasn't at all impressed with how they looked, disagreeing with Walsh's promise that they looked 'amazing, just amazing'. He thought they sang well, but he wasn't sure about their look at all, and asked Walsh to consider some changes in personnel. He wanted Filan dropped. Walsh refused to make any changes, saying he was going to remain loyal to the band members as they stood. Cowell flew home empty handed.

This wasn't the end of the matter, though. Months later, Cowell received another excited phone call from Walsh. The Irishman announced that he had made changes to the line-up of IOU, and invited Cowell back to Ireland to see the new band. When he got there, he was won over within seconds of the performance. All the doubts of his previous visit evaporated and he offered them a record deal on the spot. It was only later that he realized that the new member of the band was actually Filan, the boy he'd wanted to drop from the band. Walsh was so committed to Filan's presence that he had dyed his hair blond for the second meeting with Cowell, who now salutes Walsh for this move. All the same, the band were hastily sent off to the same stylists the Spice Girls had used for a makeover.

Meanwhile, Cowell and Walsh found some top producers and songwriters for the band to work with. Another early decision made by Cowell was to change the band's name. No more would they be known as IOU, from now on they would be Westlife. Cowell and Walsh soon found they worked together effectively and enjoyably. They share a burning ambition, smouldering charm and bubbly determination. Both also appreciate straight-talking and cheeky humour. They quickly struck up an entertaining killer rapport. At this point they were content for that rapport to be in the background of the music industry, but years later they would move it centre stage, becoming quite a double act on Saturday night television.

Westlife quickly became a formidable music act. Their first single was released in April 1999. Called 'Swear It Again', it was written by the noted songwriting partnership of Steve Mac and Wayne Hector, and reached number one in the UK, Ireland and New Zealand. Following a second Westlife number one with 'If I Let You Go', Cowell snapped up another song from the Mac/Hector partnership, and it became the ballad which to this day is synonymous with the band. Cowell had to lock the pair in his office for two hours in order to persuade them to give Westlife the song, as they had more or less promised it to someone else. Cowell made it clear that they wouldn't be allowed to leave until they agreed to give it to him. The song was called 'Flying Without Wings' and it went straight to number one.

Westlife were famous and so, increasingly, was Cowell, who was interviewed about his part in the band's success. He told the *Sunday Herald* that the pop market was currently divided, with teenagers arranging their buying habits over strictly partisan lines. There was, Cowell claimed, a '"Them and us" culture where teenagers are concerned. There are a number of groups, such as Westlife and S Club 7, who seem to appeal to a particular market age-wise, but don't have a problem retaining that fan base as it ages for a few years. Boyzone, Take That and East 17 were also similar. On the other side of the coin are young teenagers who have railed against what they see as the squeaky-clean side of pop. They prefer either more raunchy pop bands like All Saints or the more outlandishly behaved guys like Eminem or Liam Gallagher.'

Showing some of the honesty that he would soon become famous for, he admitted that he wouldn't like to see many more bands similar to his Irish wonders in the charts. 'What's wonderful about pop music is that all those elements are necessary to make it a vibrant mix. Much though I love and admire Westlife, the charts would be a dull place if the Top Thirty was filled with groups similar to them,' he continued. 'Equally so, however, after a couple of weeks the novelty of thirty indie bands dominating the charts would also soon wear off.' Recalling his own youth, he drew parallels between the nature of the pop charts back then and in the 1990s. 'The sort of good-natured conflict you have between youngsters' musical tastes is an integral part of British music and is no new thing. When I was a kid we'd all hang around the school playground with a radio, waiting to hear the weekly chart, and we'd all be bickering away about the relative merits of people like Slade, T.Rex and Gary Glitter. I don't think much has really changed.'

With the spectre of missing out on the Spice Girls still preying on his mind, Cowell also had a crack at the girl-band market with a new band called Girl Thing. He and Herbert spent nearly two years putting the five-piece together, spending an estimated £1.5 million on the development. The group – Linzi, Nikki, Michelle, Jodi and Anika – were clearly based on the Spice model. 'We're like a big gang, and we want everyone to join us,' Linzi said at their launch, adding that her hobby was 'having a laugh'. Their clothes and image were very much of the 'everyday' variety that had made the Spices so popular. The lyrics of their opening single, released in June 2000, called 'Last One Standing', appeared to include a pop at the Spice Girls: 'It's the end of an era, the start of a new day... Forget everything you've heard before, no matter how many times you hear this, you wanna hear it some more.'

Sadly, the band were not the success Cowell had hoped for. 'Obviously, not enough people wanted to buy the record,' he admitted to *The Guardian* when the debut single sold disappointingly. 'Maybe it is a bit close to "Wannabe". We wouldn't have released it if we'd known there'd be such a backlash. But this record will probably sell 100,000 in the UK, we've gone in at eight, which is fine, and we're poised to put out a much stronger song for the second record ['So You Want to Have Sex']. This is going to work for them.'

It certainly didn't work to the extent that Cowell would have liked, and Girl Thing split two years later. Jodi later told *Metro* newspaper how she was relieved by the split, and what caused it. 'I was in this manufactured band at fifteen, taken out of school, signed to a record label and flown around the world for two years. It was amazing, but I hit seventeen and thought: "I don't want to live the rest of my life in a manufactured band." It finished because the girls didn't get on – there was no other reason.' She still bumps into Cowell occasionally, as she has dated Kian Egan of Westlife. 'Most of the time, I agree with the things he says to those *X Factor* contestants,' she says. 'He doesn't say things to be nasty – he says it because he's got years of experience and knows what the business can be like.'

Despite the disappointment of Girl Thing, with the success of Westlife and Five, these were good times for Cowell professionally. However, this phenomenal success was overshadowed by an enormous tragedy in his life. When 'Swear It Again' went to number one in April 1999, it was the happiest and proudest day of his career to date. However it was also the saddest day of his life, as earlier in the day his father Eric had died from a heart attack at the family home. Eric's sudden death came as a shock to Julie, who mourned the fact that she never had a chance to say goodbye to her beloved husband. Family and close friends flocked to the house to comfort Julie and grieve over the loss of the enormously loved Eric. Cowell, meanwhile, had flown to Boston in America for an important board meeting at BMG. There, he was due to unveil Westlife to BMG managers across the globe. He was in jubilant and confident mood as he prepared to go into the meeting on a high, ready to break the news of the band's first number one to the assembled bosses.

First, though, he rang his mother to tell her the news about his band's number one. He knew there was something wrong as his mother seemed out of breath and said little; she seemed keen to bring the conversation to a swift conclusion. Her son simply concluded she must have been busy and that he had called at a bad time. Julie recalls the conversation from her end. 'It was the most awful thing,' she sighed. 'He came on so thrilled, saying, "Guess what?" Westlife were number one. It was his big break and he was over the moon. I couldn't speak. I told him that I was breathless because I'd run up the stairs. I made out that I couldn't hear him properly. He was all cock-a-hoop, and I let him go without telling him his father was dead.'

There had been much debate at the family home as to whether they should tell Cowell that his father had died. 'I knew... it was Simon's big moment,' Julie remembered. 'He was doing a promotion tour of the States and I didn't want to ruin it for him.' The local vicar, Father Martin Morgan, arrived at the family home and advised the family that Cowell should be told. 'I remember there was a big family debate as to whether they should spoil Simon's success by telling him about his father's death,' he said on *This is Your Life*. 'I managed to persuade them to ring him because he will always put his family before the business and always put his father much higher than the business.'

It was decided that Cowell must be told and the task of breaking the news fell to Nicholas. Cowell was preparing to eat breakfast in America when he took the call. 'I've got something to tell you,' Nicholas told him, the strain evident in his voice. 'It's Dad, he died today.' Cowell was shocked and devastated. He had been utterly devoted to his father and this unexpected loss knocked him for six. When he spoke to his mother he told her she was quite right to inform him about his father's death. He would never have forgiven himself, he told her, if he had continued celebrating Westlife's success while his family mourned back home in England.

Cowell's colleagues quickly rallied round. A private jet was chartered to take him from Boston to New York, where he could take Concorde home to England to join his family. To complicate matters, Concorde had an engine malfunction and was unable to fly, so Cowell had to take a normal jet home and then drive to the family home in Brighton. His mother recalls the arrival of her son. 'When he came in the front door, he was in pieces,' she recalled. 'He sobbed and sobbed.' His brother Tony has similar memories of Cowell's return. 'I really had to play the part of the older brother,' he said in an interview with the *Daily Mail*. 'You never see Simon cry, but that day he completely let go.' There were more tears at the funeral, where Tony held Cowell's hand. 'At the funeral he sobbed and sobbed. He adored his father and it meant so much that he'd been a success in his eyes.'

He took a week off work following the funeral while he grieved for his dead father. 'He was my best friend and he gave me so much good advice and I'll always remember that,' recalled Cowell later.

He suffered another bereavement that year when one of the managers of Five, Bob Herbert, died. Herbert had come agonizingly close to managing two of the biggest British pop acts of the twentieth century. He had helped nurture Bros, but couldn't sign a contract with them until they were eighteen, at which point Tom Watkins stepped in and snapped them up. He then put together the band that eventually became the Spice Girls, but lost their signature to Simon Fuller. So when he and Cowell put Five together, they were determined to get it right. 'Up until then, no one knew that we'd put the Spice Girls together, and suddenly it hit the press: the media went crazy for the auditions,' he said in *Five: The Official Book*. 'The headlines read, "Spice Boys Wanted, Boy Power!" We were being talked about on every TV and radio station. Thousands of lads turned up. It was madness.' Herbert died instantly when he lost control of his red MGF sports car in Windsor Great Park, Berkshire in August 1999. Driving in heavy rain, he spun out of control and was struck by another car, crashing into a fence. 'Bob Herbert worked closely with many people here in the past two years,' Cowell told the BBC. 'Everyone here respected him greatly, and he was always the perfect gentleman. He will be missed by all of us as a colleague and, more importantly, as a friend.' Later that year, he named Herbert's death as the music industry's greatest low point of the year during an interview with trade magazine *Music Week*.

The joy of reaching number one with 'Swear It Again' seemed a distant memory in the wake of his father's death. With the sort of strange irony that life regularly creates, Eric was the man who recommended to Cowell that 'Swear It Again' should be selected as Westlife's first single. 'Yes he did,' Cowell confirmed on *This is Your Life*. 'I remember playing him the record and he had a fantastic ear for music. He said, "They'll go to number one."' And they did just that with their first three singles. The fourth Westlife single was a cover of 'I Have A Dream'. Cowell had chosen it as Westlife's 1999 Christmas single. His moment of inspiration came when he went to watch the Abba musical *Mamma Mia* with his girlfriend. Not normally a fan of musicals, he was nonetheless struck with inspiration that night. He got his old friend Pete Waterman onboard to produce the single and the race for the Christmas number one was on.

Cowell and Westlife's nearest opponent in the race to top the charts came in the shape of Cliff Richard with his single 'The Millennium Prayer'. The fact that Cowell hated Richard's single (the worst song of all time, he has said) gave him an even more competitive edge. If Westlife topped the charts this time, they would have the Christmas number one, the first number one of the new millennium and their fourth consecutive chart-topper. The stakes could hardly have been higher for Cowell and his band. He had begun preparation for the chase in the autumn of 1999. 'You've got to make a decision now so retailers know what is happening,' he told *Music Week* in October of that year. 'You've got to put your promotion in place and either go for the Christmas number one or millennium number one. I think more people are going to go for the millennium number one because it is only going to happen once.'

The race for the Christmas number one became something of a media event that year. There was a lot of disapproval of Richard's record and the media had a good sneer at him. George Michael described 'The Millennium Prayer' as 'vile' and Spice Girl Mel C went further, calling it 'shit'. Naturally, Richard used all this to his advantage, painting himself as the plucky underdog, fighting against media-induced cynicism. At the time Cowell was in Mauritius, having continued a family tradition started by his father. Each Christmas, Eric had taken the family to a hot country for a holiday, and after his death Cowell continued to jet off with his mother each winter for a bit of sun, as he does to this day. As he sat in Mauritius that December, he was delighted to learn that early sales figures for 'I Have A Dream' were very healthy indeed.

At the last moment, Westlife beat Cliff Richard to the finishing line and claimed the prestigious Christmas number one. In credit to Richard, he was gracious in defeat, telling reporters, 'If I had to be knocked off the number one spot, then I couldn't be happier than for it to be Westlife that did it. It's a great song and I really like the guys.'

It had been a narrow victory for Westlife, who sold just 43,000 more copies than Richard. However, as Cowell celebrated this latest triumph, he must have reflected on where he stood in the industry. He had launched himself into the pop charts with wrestlers and Power Rangers. He had then cashed in on the popularity of a military television drama. Nothing wrong with any of that, of course, and he was enormously proud of his successes with each and every act. However, with Five and Westlife he was enjoying successive number one hits with proper pop bands, and he was in no doubt that Westlife had a huge future ahead of them.

Cowell was being hailed for his part in the Westlife success story. At the end of 1999, he was tipped by *Music Week* as their 'Executive to Watch' for 2000 by a number of interviewees, including his pal Louis Walsh and Jeremy Marsh of Telstar. Marsh gushed, 'I admire Simon Cowell of RCA. He knows exactly what he is going to do with a band – he masterminded Westlife.' In the same journal, Cowell himself discussed how 1999 had treated him. He said the high point of the year was 'Finally having a number one with Five', and that the low point professionally was the death of the band's manager Bob Herbert. The ever-competitive Cowell described his greatest frustration of the year as 'other people having hits' and named his song of the millennium as 'Mack The Knife' by Bobby Darin.

The year 2000 was another good year for Cowell and for Westlife. The Irish boy band had gone to number one with their first seven singles and then, in November 2000, they released their second album, *Coast to Coast*. In the first week of its release, the album sold 234,000 copies in the UK and went to number one, holding off the challenge of *Forever* by the Spice Girls. Cowell might have missed out on the Christmas number one two years running thanks to the Spice Girls, but finally he had his revenge. *Coast to Coast* went on to achieve multi-platinum status, selling more than 1.5 million copies. It wasn't just record sales that Westlife were excelling at at the turn of the century. The band constantly vindicated Cowell's faith in them by winning award after award. They won seven gongs at the 2000 Smash Hits Awards, including Best Band on Planet Pop, Best Album and Best Band. They were Best Band at the TV Hits Awards in the same year and the Best Male Group at the Disney Channel Kids Awards. Filan was also voted 'Most Fanciable Male' at the Smash Hits Awards. He could have afforded a wry chuckle at this fact, since it was Filan who Cowell had asked Walsh to drop from the band's original line-up because he didn't like his look.

Despite his success with bands, Cowell was still open to suggestions of television/music combinations. Having been the focal point of such commercial crossovers years earlier, he now saw that the rest of the industry had noticed how much money could be made and put aside their distaste for such ventures. However, Cowell was still usually the music industry man that television figures came to with ideas. One such approach came from Celador executive Paul Smith, who was working on a new game show for ITV called *Who Wants To Be A Millionaire* and wanted Cowell to be involved in the composition of the theme tune for the show. Cowell took Pete Waterman with him to meet Celador and the pair had a huge argument and never ended up composing the theme music for the show. However, their rapport – albeit an argumentative one – was obvious for all to see. Smith told them they would make excellent television. There's an idea, thought Cowell, storing it away in his memory bank.

At this time, Cowell came the closest he has ever been to getting married. Having been linked with pop singer Naima Belkhiati in 2000, he subsequently became engaged to a model known only as Louise (she has never publicly identified herself). He met her at a record industry bash at the turn of the century and there followed a rather disaster-ridden period. It took many months for him to arrange a date with her and then, on the evening in question, he was struck down by influenza. A second liaison was arranged for a couple of days later, but it too went badly, as this time Cowell was suffering from good old-fashioned nerves. The relationship – such as it was – broke down at this point and he didn't hear from her again for twelve months. It was at that point, having learned that Louise had become single again, that Cowell made his move. He took her for dinner and this time neither illness or shyness got in the way of their dating.

Within five months, they were getting on so well they got engaged during a holiday in New York. Cowell's friends were stunned at how suddenly it had all happened, and their doubts as to whether he had acted too hastily were confirmed soon after when the engagement was called off. Louise wanted a traditional family and Cowell was working nearly every hour God sent. Emotionally they were very close, but on a practical level things didn't look too compatible for the pair so they decided to split. Not that this was the end of the matter. Cowell and Louise got back together again, dated for another year, then split up and got back together a third time. Ultimately, they went their separate ways romantically, but remained good friends.

Cowell soon made his first appearance on television in *Sale of the Century*. The show has been a feature of television channels across the world since 1969. It combined a general knowledge quiz with a 'shopping' element, whereby contestants were given the chance to 'buy' prizes at knockdown prices. It aired on ITV between the 1970s and 1990s, and it was in the latter decade that Cowell appeared on it as a contestant. Being introduced as a record company director, the host Peter Marshall announces that Cowell 'enjoys watching motor-racing and is a keen go-kart racer.' He then asks Cowell if it was a dangerous pursuit, and a shy, softly spoken Cowell replies, 'Not really, no.' Asked if he is sure, he smiles and says, 'Positive.' Cowell then jokes that the maximum speed achievable on a go-kart is ten miles an hour, contradicting himself by then adding that they can actually go as fast as fifty miles per hour. So far, so awkward.

Having been introduced, it was time for Cowell to compete alongside his fellow contestants. The first question he answered correctly was, 'Devastasting parts of the Caribbean in 1989, what type of natural phenomenon was christened Hugo?' Cowell buzzed and said, 'A hurricane.' He then answered correctly questions about – among other things – jewellery entrepreneur Gerald Ratner, charitable music man Bob Geldof and mushrooms. At one point some male voices from the audience roared their encouragement for Cowell. 'Is that your girlfriend?' asks the presenter. 'She's got a very deep voice,' quipped Cowell. Later, as Cowell maintained his lead, the presenter told him, 'You are looking very steely and immovable over there, Simon.'

Not steely enough to win a car, though. Instead he settled for a set of kitchen utensils. There the matter would have rested had it not been for a woman called Barbara Humphreys, one of Cowell's fellow contestants on the show, who – many years later once Cowell was a household name – found the video on which she had recorded the episode. 'Watching the video now, I remember thinking Simon was quite posh and handsome,' Humphreys said in the *Sun*. 'He had a good sense of humour, but I would never have put him down as a future superstar. He prattled on a lot backstage about wanting a Fiat Uno, but it obviously wasn't the height of his ambition!'

She added that Cowell had a lot more hair back in those days and speculated that he must have had his teeth done since. 'He was very pleasant and said he was a record company director. But the main thing I remember about him is he couldn't answer one of the questions. He didn't know who Saddam Hussein was, but I suppose in 1990 a lot of people would have been the same.' It wasn't an auspicious television début and nobody watching could have predicted that the shy, gentle-voiced male contestant would go on to become a television megastar, dominating the airwaves in several countries, including the United States of America.

That, however, was exactly what he was about to do. Having noted the way that television and music could be combined to devastatingly profitable effect, he was on the brink of being centre stage as the two mediums joined together in a whole new way. An entertainment bandwagon that would be worth billions of pounds was about to hit the road, and Cowell very nearly missed the ride.

# CHAPTER FOUR

# THE IMPORTANCE OF BEING IDOL

Nowadays, Cowell is a man who absolutely basks in the glory of fame and the attention that goes with it. With his perma-tanned face, his bright white teeth and rumoured use of Botox, he is a natural on television. Between his work on *The X Factor*, *Britain's Got Talent* and *American Idol* he is rarely off our screens. Add in the chat shows and other media appearances and Cowell is a television fixture. So it comes as something of surprise to learn that when he was first offered the chance to break into television he meekly turned it down.

As the summer of 2000 drew to a close, Cowell was mulling over an interesting proposal. Over lunch at the exclusive Ivy restaurant in London's West End, he had been sounded out about a new television project. His dining companion that day was Nigel Lythgoe, a television producer with an enormous reputation. For ten years Lythgoe had commissioned and produced a raft of highly successful television programmes, including Saturday night classics such as *Gladiators* and *That's Life*. If you watched television on Saturday evenings during the 1990s, the chances are you'd have seen a show that Lythgoe was behind. The idea he put to Cowell was for another show that he hoped would have Saturday evening television viewers gripped. He had just bought the rights to the show from an Australian television company and it was to be called *Popstars*.

The programme would exploit the growing success of reality television shows and bring a pop-music twist to the genre. Advertisements would be placed in the press asking for auditionees for a new pop band. The show would film those auditions as the field was eventually whittled down from thousands to just five people, who would form the band. After that, the series would follow the band as a fly on the wall as they rehearsed, recorded and performed. With this combination of the traditional television talent show plus a fly-on-the-wall reality element, *Popstars* was set to be a hit. With Lythgoe behind it, there was every chance it would become another show that had the viewing public addicted. His question to Cowell was simple: will you be the lead judge at the auditions? Cowell was fascinated by the show and tempted to take up Lythgoe's offer. He even agreed in principle, provided he was allowed to sign the resulting pop band to his label.

However, in the days that followed, Cowell began to have second thoughts. He wondered whether he really wanted to appear on television and endure everything that goes with becoming a celebrity. Cowell also felt uncomfortable about the *Popstars* premise, and worried that showing how a pop band is put together would be dangerously akin to a magician showing how he or she does their tricks. As a man in the centre of the pop industry, he doubted whether it was right for that industry to show the public how it operates. Would the public even care, he wondered. So he phoned Lythgoe, told him he was pulling out and continued going about his regular business. At this point, it seemed that his one-and-only television appearance would be on *Sale of the Century*.

When *Popstars* launched months later, however, Cowell was blown away by its success. It was an absolute smash hit and had the entire nation talking. The judging panel had Lythgoe joined by record promoter Nicki Chapman and A&R legend Paul Adam. They judged thousands of auditionees, who ranged from the brilliant to the atrocious and everything in between. Lythgoe's witty and withering put-downs of the bad ones made him an instant talking point and he was quickly dubbed 'Nasty Nigel' for his straight-talking assessments of the hopefuls. The show was full of drama, hilarity, heartbreak and triumph. A Scottish singer called Darius Danesh became a national laughing stock for his overconfident persona, greasy ponytail, goatee beard and comical a cappella performance of the Britney Spears hit 'Baby One More Time'. Eventually, the field was reduced to ten contestants, of whom five made it through to the band. Those who didn't make it were distraught when they were told, while the lucky five were jubilant. There was suspense aplenty and tears galore. No wonder the public was hooked.

Just prior to the show being broadcast, Cowell had been feeling slightly dissatisfied with his career. He felt the industry had become somewhat stagnant and routine. What was needed, he felt, was something to shake everything up. As he sat at home watching *Popstars*, he realized that this show would do just that. He bitterly regretted not taking the chance to become one of the judges and on missing out on the rights to sign the resulting band, Hear'Say. Despite his feeling that he had made a colossal error, he carried on watching the show. His girlfriend was obsessed with *Popstars* and he enjoyed dissecting where the show was right and where it was went wrong. Essentially, he felt they had got it right, but with a few tweaks to the format he believed the show could have been even bigger. This wasn't just idle armchair commentary, though, as Cowell was already starting to think about his own programme. The man who he would get to work with him on this idea was the man he'd approached when trying to steal the Spice Girls: Simon Fuller.

Fuller was born in 1960 and went on to work at Chrysalis records, where he rose fast to become an A&R scout. In the mid-1980s he formed his own company and had a number one hit with Paul Hardcastle's song '19' about the Vietnam War. He then launched the career of singer-songwriter Cathy Dennis and kickstarted former Eurythmics singer Annie Lennox's solo career, before taking control of the all-conquering Spice Girls.

The two Simons' paths had crossed a few times since the Spice Girls. They would see each other at industry bashes and even holidayed in Mauritius at the same time one year. The more they talked, the more they hit it off. Indeed, the pair were mildly disturbed by how similarly they viewed things, right down to their favourite author, the satirical wordsmith Tom Sharpe. Their potential suitability had also been noted by others. Cowell's BMG manager Michael Griffiths had long suggested Fuller as an eligible ally for Cowell. There was an air of inevitability to all this: for the past half decade the two Simons had enjoyed enormous, but separate, success in the British pop industry. The time was fast approaching for them to work together.

At the Record of the Year Awards at the end of 2000, the two Simons agreed to meet for dinner in January. The key topic of conversation was the success of *Popstars* and how they could create their own – even better – version of the show. Nigel Lythgoe, the brains and star behind *Popstars*, had agreed to come on board, too, and with Cowell and Fuller behind the wheel, they knew they made a 'dream team'. As well as nailing down the finer creative details, they also carved up the all-important commercial considerations. Simon Fuller's 19 Entertainment company would own the television rights to the show and would manage the winner. Meanwhile, Cowell would get to sign the winner of the show, which would be called *Pop Idol*. They were keen to get the show on air as quickly as possible, in order to ride on the wave of popularity created by *Popstars*. Cowell was transfixed and enlivened by the prospect of *Pop Idol* and worked even harder than usual to make everything happen. This show, he was convinced, would be huge.

FremantleMedia was the production company signed up to develop and produce the show, alongside the Simons, and meetings were duly arranged with the commissioning honchos at ITV and the BBC. During their pitch to the formidable Claudia Rosencrantz at ITV in early 2001, Cowell was interrupted by her around 120 seconds into his presentation. He feared the interruption was going to be negative, but instead, the commissioning executive simply said, 'I'll take it.' Her straightforward acceptance showed how excited she was by the idea of the show, and she wanted it on ITV that very autumn. Rarely has a television presentation pitch gone so smoothly. The BBC subsequently made an offer themselves, but the Simons decided to go with ITV. They had offered first and, as the home of *Popstars*, it seemed natural to go with ITV for *Pop Idol*. It was game on for the new reality pop show.

Soon, the team that would put together the show was completed. Cowell would head up the judging panel, and alongside him would be his old mucker Pete Waterman, Nicki Chapman and Capital Radio DJ Neil Fox. The judging panel began to rev up for the auditions, and in the book *Pop Idol*, Waterman explains the way they intended to play it: 'You can't be soft when you say to someone "no" – because no is no. The Japanese don't have a word for "no", because it's offensive. We're here, being offensive. That's the way it is.' Chapman said, 'I know how tough it's going to be, but the only way to impress us is by enjoying the audition. We're not looking for a wallflower.' Fox, meanwhile, struck a more conciliatory note: 'I think if I had to give myself a nickname, I'd like to give myself the nickname Fair Foxy. I want to be fair. It's not about being nasty with people, it's about being honest with them.' As for Cowell, he was concise and direct. 'Listen,' he said, glaring. 'It's very simple, I'm at the auditions and I choose someone based on whether I'd choose them under normal circumstances. Entrants must rehearse, rehearse and rehearse. It's important they go to the audition and do the best they can do. They've only got once chance.'

It was going to be a dynamic judging panel. Meanwhile the behind-the-scenes team saw *Popstars* judge Nigel Lythgoe join Richard Holloway and Ken Warwick as executive producers. It was a winning combination and this team was to become the spine of further shows across the world. On the opening episode of the show, Cowell explained what they were looking for in their pop idol search. He said the winner would need to have 'the X factor'. He also explained what they were *not* looking for. 'If I had a seventeen-year-old pop star, twenty-nine stone with acne, then I think we'd have a real battle on our hands,' he told the camera. Ironically, he would throughout both series of the show be the judge who was most welcoming and supportive of larger contestants.

The audition process needed a lot of refining in the early stages of recording. The first filming took place in Manchester and at that point, after their performance, the contestants would leave the room so the judges could discuss them, then the contestant would be asked to return to the room for the verdict. This was contrary to how normal pop auditions worked, when the auditionee would be told the verdict straight after they'd performed. The *Pop Idol* auditions were quickly brought in line with the industry standard, but it still felt wrong to Cowell. It was time for a cigarette break and a chat. Cowell complained that the politeness of the judges' feedback was creating a fake atmosphere, and he insisted the panel should speak as they normally spoke in auditions – honestly and directly. This was quickly agreed and the auditions resumed. Straight talk was to be the order of the day from thereon in.

One of the first to audition under this new regime was a blond singer called Ben, whose nickname, he told the cameras, was Sexual Sharman. He certainly looked the part of a pop idol and sang 'Angel's Wings' by Westlife, one of Cowell's acts. He was confident and clearly expected to sail through, but he was in for a rude awakening. Waterman told him he sounded far too much like Westlife. 'What we didn't hear was you,' he concluded. Ben sank to his knees in despair. Cowell whispered, 'Oops,' but his eyes lit up with excitement. Fox and Chapman both gave similarly damning verdicts and Ben turned up the dramatics when he discovered he wasn't going through, throwing his sunglasses against the wall, looking as if he was on the brink of tears and kicking the wall in anger. Cowell tapped his chin throughout Ben's histrionics, and after the distraught contestant had left the room, Cowell quipped, 'I thought he took it quite well.' The panel burst out laughing at his sarcastic, perfectly timed remark.

The tone was set for the series: the judges would offer honest advice and were not afraid to be direct. The most direct of them all was Cowell, who quickly became known as Mr Nasty, the villain of the show. No episode was complete without one of his withering verdicts. When a contestant told him she had taken singing lessons, he implored her to 'sue the teacher'. He told another, 'I think you bored everyone on the panel,' and another, 'I'm afraid to say that really hurt my ears.' He would criticize their choice of song, their vocals and even what they were wearing. A correspondent to the *Sun* wrote that Cowell should make a New Year's resolution to be less rude. 'Mr Nasty Simon Cowell should make a resolution to be more civil and less intimidating to contestants. Constructive criticism is acceptable, downright rudeness isn't,' stormed Neil Taylor of Oxford.

An early auditionee was a young man from Bradford called Gareth Gates. The seventeen-year-old had spiky black hair and perfect boy-band looks. When he arrived, Fox asked him to introduce himself. 'My name is,' he began, then struggled for some time to complete the sentence. Finally, after an excruciating delay, he completed, 'Gareth Gates.' He then sang 'Flying Without

Wings', the song Cowell and Westlife had enjoyed a huge hit with. As his angelic voice sang the opening words, Cowell was looking at the floor, but once Gates's voice emerged, Cowell's eyes slowly looked up at the singer with a barely suppressed look of awe. It was a beautiful performance and had the judges enthralled and charmed. Cowell held his hand up and said, 'OK, I'm going to stop you there. You are one hundred per cent coming to London for the next audition,' he continued, praising the singer's bravery.

When the audition was broadcast, viewers got the impression that Cowell had never met Gates before. However, according to another contestant, this was not the case. Andrew Derbyshire, who made the final fifty on the show and has since become a musical theatre star, appearing in *We Will Rock You* and as Joseph in the touring production of *Joseph and the Amazing Technicolor Dreamcoat*, says both he and Gates had met Cowell prior to *Pop Idol*, and that he had urged the pair to enter the show. 'We did an audition, me and Gareth, for a boy band way before *Pop Idol* and this man who turned up was called Simon Cowell, someone that I'd never heard of before,' he told the *Financial Times*. 'I was actually sat in his office in BMG and he told me about this new show called *Pop Idol* and could I enter and he hoped I would, and Gareth was there at the time.' Gates did indeed enter and in him, Cowell felt, the show had a potential winner.

Another contestant who thought he was a potential winner was David Graham. He was an experienced singer, and was therefore pulled out for a special feature in the editing. He was shown performing at schools and other venues around the country, which he had been doing for the past five years. Once in the audition room, he sang 'I Believe I Can Fly'. As Graham completed his performance by repeating the line, 'I believe I can fly,' Cowell said, 'I don't... believe he can fly.' He added that he thought his outfit was five or ten years out of date. Now Graham looks back on his *Pop Idol* experience and confirms that it was Cowell and the fellow judges who ruled the roost. 'No matter what the production company behind the show think of you, it's all about the judges,' says Graham, who reauditioned in series two. 'I remember not really knowing much about Cowell in the first series. He told me he thought I sounded too much like the artist whose song I was performing. On the second season he really stuck up for me against the other judges because of my age, although he wouldn't believe I had performed as many of my own shows as I had.'

A mixed encounter with Cowell, then, for Graham. However, he recalls his brushes with Mr Nasty in an essentially respectful tone. 'People are always going to judge others by what they see rather than the person underneath. I personally think he's the most honest judge there has been on any reality TV show of this kind, although, like everyone, I would say he sometimes gets it wrong, but nobody's perfect.'

The other judges were rarely as cutting as Cowell, with the possible exception of Waterman. An early quip of his to a contestant was, 'The only pop you can do is "pop off"!' Chapman and Fox, on the other hand, were normally constructive, but Cowell wasn't averse to interrupting them as they gave their verdicts. When Chapman told one less-than-impressive auditionee that although he hadn't sung well, he seemed to enjoy singing, Cowell interrupted, 'But, Nicki, enjoyment is normally two-way. He might have enjoyed it, I didn't.' She couldn't help but smile at Cowell's concise and direct assessment.

The second round of auditions was held in London. At the beginning of the proceedings, the judges held a Q&A session with the remaining hundred contestants. As they arrived one by one, they got varied reactions from the hopefuls. Cowell was booed but shrugged it off. He told the contestants that the person who went on to win the show would be, quite simply, 'the most famous person in the country.' As he prepared for the opening episodes of the show to be transmitted, Cowell reflected on the new fame that *he* would acquire through *Pop Idol*. He was in no doubt that the show was going to be an enormous success, especially as *Popstars* had transfixed the viewing nation the previous year. With improvements in the *Pop Idol* format, such as the addition of public voting, Cowell was convinced that this show would be even bigger. Add to the mix the fact that he was set to become the show's biggest talking point, thanks to his tough verdicts, and Cowell could see that he was headed for an unprecedented level of media scrutiny, the likes of which he'd never encountered before. He was particularly concerned about his romantic history hitting the newspapers. Cowell had seen what celebrities faced from the tabloid press in particular through the experiences of his artists, and he was determined to have as much control as possible over how he was reported.

Cowell insisted on getting the best protection money could buy, so he turned to the man widely considered to be the best at media manipulation, Max Clifford. Born in Surrey in 1943, Clifford was a journalist for a short time before entering the world of publicity at EMI, where he helped promote The Beatles in their early years. He eventually formed his own public relations agency, where he represented such stars as Muhammad Ali, Marlon Brando, Jimi

Hendrix and Frank Sinatra. More recently, he has become the master of press management, preventing unflattering stories about his clients being printed and placing stories on their behalf. A large proportion of the big stories the tabloid press print about celebrities have appeared because of his direct involvement. However, he is also responsible for a lot of the stories the public doesn't read. There are few people in the world better equipped than Clifford to hush-up a story a newspaper is planning to break.

On the Max Clifford Agency website, there is a 'case study' page outlining how Clifford and Cowell worked together. 'He knew that his eye for the ladies left him in danger of being perfect kiss-and-tell fodder,' says the text. 'Clifford's unique combination of protection and publicity helped control his image and cement his place as one of the world's most successful music moguls,' it continues. That relationship began when Cowell visited Clifford at his New Bond Street offices in 2001. The pair had a semi-formal chat, and Cowell explained why he felt he needed Clifford's help. The agent wasn't immediately convinced, but he nonetheless agreed to work with Cowell. When he told his new client what his fees were, Cowell was gobsmacked – the lowest rate was £10,000 per month – but he stuck with his hunch and the pair decided to work together.

A great insight into how well Cowell and Clifford operated was gained by oddball television presenter Louis Theroux. He fronted a series of shows called *When Louis Met...*, in which he followed a celebrity around for a few days. Clifford was one such subject, although the show turned into *When Louis Met Max Clifford and Simon Cowell*, as Cowell appeared so often during filming. Cowell was a subject of discussion from the opening minutes of the show and first appeared during a Clifford-arranged visit to a hospital by the band Westlife. The previous day, the *Sport* newspaper had printed a story about a romp between Cowell and a Page Three model, and the three men exchanged banter about the story. 'Simon's been a busy boy for the past twenty years, and now he's become a celebrity, his past is catching up with him,' Clifford told Theroux. 'There are lots [of women] in his past,' he added. 'There have been four in the past few weeks [trying to sell their story].' Cowell told Theroux he hadn't yet read the *Sport* story, but after stepping outside to read it, he reappeared laughing and said, 'Every word was true.' He was, he added, particularly amused by her revelation that he folds his socks before having sex.

Theroux and Cowell later had a one-to-one chat about his relationship with Clifford. 'He does some publicity for me – or more importantly lack of publicity – for me,' Cowell told the interviewer. 'It's not specific stories, but if you're out there on your own at nine o'clock on a Sunday night and you get a call from a reporter, you've got to have someone to phone. He's been able to confirm that certain things aren't true and it's better coming from Max than it is from me.' Theroux's curiosity was not yet assuaged, and back at Clifford's New Bond Street office, he confronted the publicist about a nagging suspicion he had about Cowell. 'This is a little sensitive, but I've got to level with you about it,' he said. 'I always thought Simon was gay, and yet you're talking about kiss-and-tells with women. Is he gay?' Clifford replied 'No,' and then admitted that he wouldn't say Cowell was gay even if he were. Theroux still wasn't satisfied, so he pushed the point, saying, 'He *is* gay, Max, isn't he?' Clifford deflected the tension with a joke: 'He said exactly the same about you.' Later in the day, Cowell arrived at Clifford's offices and Theroux confronted him directly about his sexuality. 'The word on the street is that you're gay,' Theroux said. 'I deny it,' Cowell replied, laughing off the suggestion.

Later in the programme, Theroux confronted Clifford over a story that had appeared in the tabloid press about a sexual liaison between Cowell and Georgina Law, a lap-dancer from the Spearmint Rhino nightclub. Theroux pointed out that this was a convenient story for Clifford, given that both Cowell and Spearmint Rhino were clients of his. Clifford insisted to Theroux that it was a genuine story about a genuine relationship. Theroux then turned the screw on Clifford, saying, 'You told [a member of his television crew] that they hadn't had sex. Why can you tell her off camera, but you can't tell me on camera?' he asked. The crew member then confirmed to Clifford that he had told her Cowell and Law had not had sex and that he had also admitted that he arranged for photographs to be taken of the pair 'appearing to be a couple'. Clifford said, 'Of course I've done that. I orchestrated the whole thing.' Theroux told the publicist, 'You're quite defensive.' Towards the end of the show, Clifford told Theroux that in the previous week he had prevented the publication of twenty stories about Cowell. They ranged, he said, 'from the sublime to the ridiculous'. The show was an entertaining and illuminating insight into how Clifford operates on Cowell's behalf.

As Cowell explained in *I Don't Mean to Be Rude, But...*, Clifford and he became close friends through their work together. When he won a major television award in 2004, he thanked only two people: his mother, Julie, and Clifford. Clifford also claims that Cowell has vowed to name his first child after him. Clifford

Cheers: in this early photo with brother Nicholas, Simon (left) has already perfected his air of sophistication.

A nineteen-year-old Cowell in Antigua in 1979, with then family friend Melissa Zimmelstern.

A young Cowell relaxes on holiday.

Cowell's former girlfriend Sinitta was the first act to be signed to Fanfare Records, the label he formed with Iain Burton.

Primetime TV success: the first series of *Pop Idol* in 2001 catapulted Cowell to fame, along with other judges (from l-r) Pete Waterman, Nicki Chapman and Neil Fox.

All smiles: Simon surrounded by contestants from the second series of *Pop Idol*, including eventual winner Michelle McManus (far left) and wild card Susanne Manning (third from left).

Mr Nice Guy? With fellow *American Idol* judges Randy Jackson and Paula Abdul and presenter Ryan Seacrest.

From scary judge to scary movies: Cowell landed a cameo role in *Scary Movie 3*.

At the *Simpsons Movie* screening in 2004. Can you spot the real Cowell?

No stopping him now: fellow judge Louis Walsh jokingly restrains Cowell at the launch of *The X Factor* in 2004.

The 2008 line-up of judges and presenters – including new addition Cheryl Cole (centre).

The ultimate accessory: Cowell steps out with former Miss Nude UK and Page 3 girl Jackie St Claire at the BRIT Awards in 2002.

Cowell's ex-girlfriend (and former Page 3 stunner) Georgina Law in 2002.

Cowell shares a close relationship with his mother Julie. Here she accompanies him to the 2005 Varlety Club Awards, along with old flame Sinitta.

Romance in the sun: Cowell in the Caribbean with his former long-term girlfriend, Terri Seymour, over Christmas 2003.

Packing a punch: a music industry heavyweight, Simon's ambition has seen him achieve enormous wealth and worldwide recognition.

watched most episodes of *Pop Idol* as they were broadcast and would think nothing of phoning Cowell afterwards if he thought he had gone too far with his verdicts. His honesty extended beyond that, to helping Cowell remember how good his life was. After Cowell became the victim of a slew of kiss-and-tell stories, he moaned to Clifford about the pitfalls of his new-found fame. 'You know what your problem is?' Clifford responded. 'You're taking yourself too seriously. Think of all the good things that have happened to you over the past few months.' He also arranged for Cowell to make his first chat-show appearance on *The Frank Skinner Show* and, knowing his client was nervous, he brought some friends and family along to the studio to distract him. Cowell had a good asset in Clifford, one that would come in handy as his *Pop Idol* fame reached ever higher proportions.

When the show reached the middle of the filming schedule, it was suggested that there should be no more judges' comments. At this stage of the proceedings, the public vote would decide which contestants went through and which were eliminated. Therefore, the producers felt, there should be no more involvement or comments from the judges. Cowell had other ideas, though, and he told the producers they were being 'idiots'. He insisted that the judges were the heart of the show, providing much of its dramatic tension. The producers stuck to their guns, though, and took Cowell out to lunch in a bid to bring him round to their way of thinking. Cowell continued to argue with them, telling them it would be a 'big mistake' to end the judges' involvement. He became even more convinced he was right when he and some friends watched the show being filmed at London's Criterion

Theatre with less involvement from the judges. He had watched several episodes of the show with the same circle of friends and he noticed that they paid less attention to the Criterion episode. ITV executive Claudia Rosencrantz agreed with Cowell that the show lost something when the judges weren't central to the action, and it was decided that the judges should remain until the end of the show. Cowell's performances during the remainder of the show would handsomely vindicate this decision. His centrality to the appeal of *Pop Idol* only increased as the shows went live and the public vote was introduced.

One contestant who had an interesting interaction with Cowell during the middle of the series was sixteen-year-old Olly Manson. Prior to entering *Pop Idol*, Manson had had little experience of performing, though he had sung karaoke. So why did he enter? 'My mum forced me to do it,' he replies, smiling. At his first audition, Manson had caused something of a rumpus amongst the judges. Waterman told him he had 'a good little pop voice', but Cowell insisted that Manson was boy-band material and not right as a solo artist. Sparks flew between the two judges while Manson watched, somewhat bemused. 'You only find out afterwards how it's all staged,' he says now. 'It's all for television. We were pretty raw [in series one]. I don't think any of the contestants knew what they were doing. We were all just going with the flow.'

This meant that what went on during filming was often at odds with what was eventually broadcast. Manson, for instance, was voted out of the show at the end of his first audition, contrary to what viewers were later shown. 'That first audition, I didn't actually get through, but they edited it really well to make it look like I did,' he says. 'Basically, Pete Waterman said yes, but the three other judges said no. However, Simon Cowell had told me, "You'd fit in very well to a boy band, give me a call." But when I left the auditions, nobody gave me Simon's number. Then a few weeks later I got a phone call from the producers. They said, "Why haven't you given Simon Cowell a call?" I said, "Because nobody gave me his number." They then told me, "We've been reconsidering your audition and we'd like you to re-join the show."'

So it was back in front of the cameras for Manson, who once again got Waterman's backing in the next round. 'It was nice, but then after the show he did nothing to follow it up, so I think again it was all for the camera rather than actual belief in me. Perhaps I'm just being cynical?' The following round was filmed at the Criterion Theatre, and the second day of filming was 11 September 2001. As al-Qaeda attacked America, the *Pop Idol* hopefuls were unaware of the unfolding tragedy. As they waited backstage at the theatre, it was Cowell who broke the news to them about what was happening across the ocean. 'I remember Simon came round with two of the producers and he told us what was going on in America,' says Manson. 'He said, "You're not going to believe this, but some planes have flown into the Twin Towers in New York." Everybody thought he'd gone mad. Then after the day's audition we all sat in the hotel lobby on Tottenham Court Road, watching the footage on the news on big screens.' Cowell had been stunned by the day's events in America. He had been told the news by Nigel Lythgoe, who took him to one side and explained what was going on. Cowell's initial reaction had been to cancel the day's filming. Unconfirmed reports suggested that London, too, might be about to face a similar terror attack. They did their best to get through the day's filming, then Cowell returned to his house with Lythgoe, where they watched the news reports and realized that there were bigger things than reality pop shows.

Manson had now reached the final fifty, where he took another volley of criticism from Cowell. However, despite his tender years, he took the feedback in good humour. 'I didn't sing very well that night, so I think that what Simon said was actually right,' he shrugged. After Cowell had offered his damning verdict, fellow judge Neil Fox leapt to Manson's defence. 'He hasn't killed anyone, he's come here to sing,' he said to Cowell, who later said he felt Fox had been bottling these sentiments up for several weeks. 'I looked into his eyes and he wasn't amused,' Cowell says in the official *Pop Idol* book. However, Manson said the disagreement between Cowell and Fox was not all it seemed. 'It was purely a television row,' he insists. 'The following week it was suggested that they'd fallen out during the row, but I know that at the end of my week's show Simon and Foxy were absolutely fine, laughing and joking about the whole thing. The fall-outs are all for television. But it was quite funny, I suppose.'

Although he had been voted out, Manson later went to the Wembley studios to watch some of the subsequent live shows. He lived nearby in Stanmore and wanted to cheer on the contestants, some of whom he'd become close to. There, he bumped into Cowell, and once more he found him to be the opposite of his on-screen persona. 'He was really nice,' says Manson. 'He never offered me anything concrete, but he was encouraging. He told me never to give up, you're only young. I remember he was also nice to my friends and to my mum. He said some lovely things about me to them. He was nice about me as a person, and said I was a really nice guy. He also told them he'd never met anyone of my age who took criticism like I did. It just didn't upset me, any of the criticism he gave me.' Indeed, throughout his time on the show, Manson says, he had a fair amount of off-camera contact with the judges. He found more than one contrast in how they behaved on and off screen. 'They were all really nice off camera, apart from Nicki Chapman,' he says, adding that he found her 'cold'. And who was the most pleasant? None other than nasty Simon. 'He was the nicest one out of the lot,' he says firmly. 'Really friendly. He likes it if people can take his criticism well. He respects people for that.'

Another contestant who responded to Cowell's criticism in an as yet unprecedented way was Berkshire boy Will Young. Thus far he'd enjoyed an understated journey through the competition. He was the final contestant to be auditioned in the first phase, where he sang 'Blame it on the Boogie' by the Jackson Five. 'I thought your vocal was good,' said Chapman. 'But I didn't like your moves at all, I've got to be honest.' Foxy compared Young's audition to 'a pleasant cheddar, rather than a stinky stilton', while Waterman was positive, as was Cowell. He asked Young, 'Does this mean a lot to you?' Then he confirmed that he was going through: 'You're a good-looking boy, you've got a nice voice. We'll see you through to the next round.' However, it had been a borderline decision. Earlier in the day, a producer had told the judges that thus far they'd put through more girls than boys. Therefore the judges were encouraged to give borderline male singers the benefit of the doubt for the rest of the day. Cowell wasn't overly impressed by Young at this point; the only thing about him he found memorable was his resemblance to Howard Donald from Take That. However,

Lythgoe encouraged him to put Young through from the wings, so through he went. That's how close the show came to eliminating the eventual winner at the first hurdle.

It was only during the second round of the competition that Young began to make an impression. He sang 'Fast Love' by George Michael at the Criterion Theatre and was filmed chatting with Ant and Dec as they interviewed him about keeping a diary. Other contestants were certainly making more of an impression than the softly spoken boy from Berkshire as the shows featuring the final fifty were broadcast. All of that was about to change however. On the evening of the fourth heat of the second phase of the series, Cowell arrived at Teddington Studios in a bad mood. Young was the final contestant to sing on the night, and he sang The Doors classic 'Light My Fire'. When he'd finished, Cowell was less than complimentary: 'I had a vision of Sunday lunch, and after Sunday lunch you say to your family "I'm now going to sing a song for you." Distinctly average, I'm afraid. I just thought it was totally normal in the context of the show. I honestly didn't think it was good enough.'

Chapman urged Young to respond to Cowell's criticism, and he did just that, telling Cowell he'd been 'dying to say something back'. 'I think it's nice that you've given an opinion on this show – in previous shows you haven't, you've just projected insults and it's been terrible to watch.' Back in the green room, the other contestants stood up to listen closely to Young's words, which were being broadcast to them via a monitor. 'It's your opinion,' continued Young calmly. 'I don't agree with it. I don't think you could ever call that average. But it is your opinion and I respect that.' It was a measured and dignified response, and Cowell had little option but to respond politely, saying, 'You are a gentleman, sir.' Cowell's relatives later said they knew he was feeling uncomfortable during Young's retort when they noticed him stick out his bottom lip, a familiar habit of his when he feels under pressure.

Young then returned to the green room to a hero's welcome from his fellow contestants. He joked that he had felt compelled to answer back because his father would have wanted him to do so. 'You're not taking that, my boy,' joked Young in a funny accent. 'Annabel [Young's mother], get the shotgun.' Young became something of a national hero for answering Cowell back. It had been a wise and expertly executed move to stand up to Mr Nasty in so polite a fashion, and his plan succeeded. Young won that evening's show with 41.5 per cent of the public vote. Only two contestants – Rosie Ribbons and Gareth Gates – had won a larger percentage of the vote during this round. Young had propelled himself into the reckoning to win the show thanks to his words with Cowell. Now it was down to Cowell to respond sensibly, and the next time he saw Young at the live shows, he did just that.

With the final ten decided, the show moved to larger studios in Wembley. Here, each Saturday night, the finalists would sing live in front of a studio audience while being watched by millions at home. The judges would offer their comments on each performance, but once more it would be the public who decided who went through each week. They would vote for their favourite performance, and the singer with the least votes would be eliminated. *Pop Idol* fever increased each week as the public became more and more gripped by the show. On the first of the live shows, Ant and Dec asked the judging panel whether they would be more measured in their feedback, given that they had a live studio audience sitting behind them. 'Yeah we're going to be really nice to everyone tonight,' joked Cowell. Some chance of that, even though, as Fox pointed out, he was within 'spitting distance' of the contenders' relatives.

The first singer to perform in the live finals was a young man called Korben, who sang and received praise for his performance of 'A Different Corner' from Fox and Chapman, although the latter judge criticized his outfit. Then it was time for Waterman's verdict. 'Uh-oh, get ready for the boos,' he said. 'I thought it was terrible. Didn't like it at all. I don't think you're my pop idol.' Cowell turned on Korben's outfit and performance, concluding, 'I don't know how well you're going to do in this competition.' It was clear that the judges were going to be central figures in the live shows and that they weren't going to be any less gentle with the contestants. Up until then, Korben had been one of the favourites to win the competition, but he was mauled by Waterman and Cowell on the night.

That evening's show was the first time that Cowell and Will Young had appeared on screen together since their famous exchange at Teddington Studios. Young sang 'Until You Come Back to Me', by Aretha Franklin. Waterman heaped praise on him, saying, 'I actually think you have the most unique voice I have heard in twenty years. Simon and me just sat here and said, "This kid is fantastic." You are fantastic.' Cowell began his feedback by asking Young, 'First question, has your dad got his shotgun with him? I have to say, William, you more than anyone, you humbled me last time. I watched it back and I realized I'd made a huge mistake in what I said. I thought the way you handled yourself was with dignity. That's what makes this competition so fantastic. The public voted against big mouth and I'm delighted for you.

You did brilliant, congratulations.' Both Young and Cowell had done very well out of the Teddington showdown. Young became a national hero for standing up to Mr Nasty, while Cowell was subsequently given a chance to show his humble side to the nation. Everyone was a winner, apart from Korben, who was the first to be voted out. Cowell denies suggestions that Korben was voted out by the public because of his homosexuality. 'I don't think that had anything to do with it. I would have liked him to have lasted a little longer because I thought he was a very good singer.' Korben's early exit surprised Cowell. He realized that the competition wasn't going to be anywhere near as predictable as he had previously imagined.

Then came a twist that served Cowell and the show well. Rik Waller, a controversial contestant due to his enormous figure, fell ill with a sore throat and was unable to perform. He was given a week to recover and Darius Danesh – who finished third in Waller's week of the final fifty phase – was lined up as standby in case Waller couldn't return. Conspiracy theories and press speculation mounted over alternative reasons for Waller's potential departure. His father then placed a story in the *Sun* saying that nothing short of a miracle would bring him back to our screens on *Pop Idol*. As for Cowell, he received reports from people behind the scenes that Waller was developing quite an ego. 'You always get the best information from the make-up artists,' he said in the *Pop Idol* book. 'They were the ones who alerted me to Rik.'

Consequently, Danesh was reinstated in the show. It was a remarkable comeback for Danesh, from national laughing stock on *Popstars* to comeback kid on *Pop Idol*. To mark the turnaround, he returned with shorter hair, a clean-shaven face and a whole new energy. Cowell had mixed feelings about Danesh. On the one hand he found him cheesy and embarrassing, but on the other, Cowell's naturally good-hearted admiration for anyone who's a trier meant he was fond of the singer's indefatigable spirit. It was a major turn-up for the books, since even Chapman had warned Danesh against entering *Pop Idol*.

Following the departure of Korben, the next contestant to leave was Jessica Garlick, a likeable Welsh singer who had distinguished herself earlier in the competition by her obsession with Pete Waterman. Cowell found her a bit too safe, and noted in his book that when she subsequently entered the Eurovision Song Contest, 'she didn't win that either'. As the live shows continued, Cowell and the other judges were as entertaining as ever. In the third week of the live shows, the contestants sang Burt Bacharach songs. Waterman told Young, 'The bad news is you're not a pop idol.' As Young's face sank and the audience began to boo, Waterman smiled and added, 'The good news is, you're a superstar!'

If any judge came close to rivaling Cowell for entertainment value, it was Waterman. The pair worked together perfectly on screen, as had been predicted all those years ago. However, a storm was brewing between them. Cowell was criticized by Waterman for his less-than-glowing review of Danesh's performance one week, but Cowell was quick to defend himself. 'I have supported him throughout this competition,' he protested. 'If we're not allowed to put an opinion over, then what is the point of us being here?' Waterman bit back. 'I disagree,' he snapped. 'This is *Pop Idol*, not "teen idol". I think age is an issue with you. You don't understand Darius. He sang the song as good as Nat King Cole. He was brilliant!'

It was playing to the gallery for sure, and Waterman received hearty applause from the studio audience. Cowell had the last word, though, telling Waterman, 'Your problem is that you get too emotionally involved.' Danesh then responded, telling the panel, 'Thank you for your comments. One of the reasons I'm here is to get your criticisms. They're constructive. But, Simon, I think you need to bring your waistband down a notch because it might be restricting the blood flow to your head.' To Cowell's credit, he managed to laugh and take the comeback on the chin. He has always believed that reality shows only work if the contestants feel empowered enough to answer back when the judges criticize them. The Cowell/Waterman exchange was another memorable moment in *Pop Idol* history. 'What were Pete and Simon going on about this week,' asked Lythgoe on ITV2's sister show, *Pop Idol Extra*. With his tongue firmly in his cheek he went on, 'As the executive producer of the programme, I will have to reprimand both of them. I am sick of listening to their petty arguments. They need to realize that this show is not about them, but about the talent in front of them. Simon is, of course, allowed his opinion, and Pete is allowed to disagree with it. But they're turning into a slightly senile, bickering old couple that didn't have the courage to get divorced twenty years ago.' Fox was asked about the controversy and was similarly bitchy. He said, 'Those two are like a couple of old battleaxes.' As Waterman revealed in the official *Pop Idol* book, it wasn't only on camera that the pair disagreed. 'The show got very heated at times off-screen, nothing to what you saw on-screen. Simon is passionate about the show, particularly about his view of who should win, and I don't agree. I think it's down to the public. I don't believe judges should guide the public vote, saying,

"You are the pop idol."' As for Cowell's accusation that Waterman got too emotionally involved, the producer roared, 'Don't fall for that line. Simon is just trying to be a smart-arse. Simon is far more involved than me.'

Cowell was increasingly coming under fire, not just for his blunt criticisms of the contestants, but for his partisan backing of Gareth Gates. Throughout the competition he passionately supported the young Yorkshireman. In a press conference he was asked who he thought would win, and rather than refuse to take sides, Cowell backed Gates to land the title. *Pop Idol Extra* presenter Kate Thornton took issue with this: 'As a judge, should you have said that?' she asked him. 'Probably not,' he admitted. 'Naughty boy!' she scolded. Cowell is quick to defend himself over how he handled his relationship with Gates. 'I was the first person who criticized him when he gave a weak performance, and the others agreed,' he says in the *Pop Idol* book. 'At the end of the day, you have to do this job as a human being, and if you think one person is better than the others, you have to say it.' Well, he was quite happy to say it about Gates. His verdicts on Gates's performances included, 'Gareth, two words: pop idol.' He also told Gates one week 'You're going to have a number one hit with that song.' A comment that led some viewers to complain that Cowell was being presumptive.

As the weeks went by, so more contestants left. Train driver Aaron Bayley, who Cowell dubbed 'the people's champion' was the third contestant voted out, which left the dotty Laura Doherty; the Welsh wonder Rosie Ribbons, who murdered 'The Winner Takes it All' in Abba week, and Hayley Evetts, who Cowell memorably told, 'You're sooooooooo sexy'. The following week, the reality of the show hit home for Cowell. He and Waterman had squabbled off air (Waterman sarcastically snapped, 'The people at home like [your] pearls of wisdom, Simon'), but it was when the results came through that Cowell felt emotional. Young Zoe Birkett came bottom in the voting, sparking a wave of upset. She and Gates had become close during the competition and the Yorkshire boy was inconsolable. The emotion spread through the studio and hit Cowell as much as anyone. It felt as though *Pop Idol*'s unofficial mascot had been voted out.

As the show reached its closing stages, Cowell backed off from being too harsh in his assessments. He felt that for the contestants to reach the very final weeks, they clearly deserved to be there. In any case, he believed that if he were to criticize contestants who had become so loved by the nation, he would be in real trouble. 'I think, to be honest, if I went for one of them now I would be assassinated. It's self-preservation at this point.' There was a tangible tension in the air as the show neared its grand finale. With the elimination of young Birkett, the semi-final saw Gates, Young and Danesh compete on an extraordinarily tense evening. The theme of the week was 'judges' choice', which meant the judging panel would select the two songs each contestant sang. There was controversy over the fact that Gates was given 'Flying Without Wings' to sing when he had already performed it twice during the competition. In the end it was an emotional night that saw Danesh eliminated. He had claimed 1.2 million of the 5.8 million votes, but that wasn't enough to save him, and he bowed out saying, 'This is not the end, this is just the beginning.'

Reflecting on these closing weeks of filming, Cowell said it was a draining time for him. 'I found the last two weeks very stressful,' he admitted. 'I think we all took it a bit too seriously at one point.' His clash with Waterman had increased the tension. 'I was sitting thinking that I was nervous about what I was going to say – not because of the way the public was going to perceive me, but because one of the three judges was going to jump down my throat. Then I thought, Fuck it, if they want to have a go at me, they should have a go at me.'

One stressful occasion was a trip Cowell took to Olympic Studios in Barnes in west London with the final three contestants (prior to Darius's elimination), so that each of them could record a winners' single. It had been decided that the single would be a double-A-side of two tracks, 'Evergreen' and 'Anything Is Possible'. *Pop Idol* cameras filmed the day, and viewers were shown a glimpse of an awkward exchange between Cowell and Danesh. The Scot felt the song was entirely unsuitable for his range and complained to Cowell. 'You've just got to try and not give up,' said Cowell. Danesh was furious at what he felt was Cowell's patronizing attitude. Cowell later did a piece-to-camera for the show and said, 'Perhaps [Danesh] is hiding his insecurities.' Cowell's discomfort wasn't helped by the fact that while he was discussing all this with Danesh, he choked on the apple he was eating. As for the single, Cowell was delighted with the double-A-side choice. 'If it's not a number one hit I'm going to eat my very high-waisted trousers,' he said, smiling.

There was a more heated debate between Danesh and Cowell the following day. Danesh had been given the Rick Astley song 'Never Gonna Give You Up' to sing at that weekend's semi-final, but he was unhappy with the choice and wanted to sing 'You've Lost That Lovin' Feeling'. 'I hear you've been causing trouble again,' Cowell told Danesh when he heard about this. 'What is it this time?' The singer explained that he felt 'You've Lost That Lovin' Feeling' was a more suitable song for him, and he even performed it in front of Cowell to make his point. The judge stood with his arms folded and restated his insistence that Danesh should not sing his choice. Words were exchanged and Cowell left the studio, saying, 'No, you're not singing that. I've got to go.' Danesh caught up with Cowell later and confronted him once more, saying he would refuse to do the show if he was forced to sing 'Never Gonna Give You Up'. Eventually a compromise was reached and Danesh sang 'Make It Easy On Yourself' instead. Not that it was enough to save him, as we have seen.

His departure set up a final between Young and Gates. It was a spectacular night of television. In many ways, the final two – Gates and Young – vindicated Cowell's input into the show. He had backed Gates from the start, and his contribution to Young's success was less direct but no less important. When Young had answered Cowell back, his popularity rocketed. It's true that Young's voice played a part in his journey, but he remained the boy who bit back at big mouth. Lest we forget, the production team originally didn't want judges to be involved in the final stages of the series. Had Cowell not got his way and had the judges' roles reinstated, Young would never have had the chance to answer Cowell back, and it's arguable that without that incident he would not have become so popular. Yet here he was, in the final alongside Cowell's favourite, Gates. All week, the pair fought an election-style campaign for votes. Both parties were given 'battle buses' to travel round the country canvassing support for the Saturday night showdown. The tabloid press devoted their front pages to the show on the morning of the final. Cowell's predictions of how big *Pop Idol* would become had proved spot on. It was to be quite a night.

Gates was widely tipped to win, but even though that was Cowell's preferred outcome, he had a sneaking feeling that Young would emerge on top. He arrived at the Wembley studios at 3 p.m. and watched the two finalists rehearse. At this point, Cowell changed his mind and decided that Gates would win the final. He believed the Yorkshireman had more self-belief than Young, who Cowell felt had lost some of his oomph. The same could be said of the judges, as Cowell detected a real feeling of anxiety in the air. Gone was the banter they'd enjoyed during previous rehearsals, and instead there was a tension about the proceedings. When he spoke to Waterman, his fellow judge didn't respond. At this stage, Cowell felt the evening was going to be a disappointment and he couldn't wait for it all to be over. His mood wasn't helped when, during Young's rehearsal of 'Light My Fire', the pyrotechnics misfired and flames hit one of the cameras.

When the show kicked off that evening, the mood was far more upbeat. The judges were all dressed up in black tie, with Waterman and Fox sporting bow-ties to top off their outfits while Cowell opted for an open shirt with his dinner jacket. As the show started broadcasting, Ant and Dec had some banter with the panel. 'Can I just say you look sensational tonight,' said Dec, mimicking one of Chapman's favourite sayings, 'the camera *loooves* you.' Cowell chipped in, referring to an earlier piece of memorable feedback he had given contestant Hayley Evetts: 'Are we *sooooooooo* sexy?' Ant and Dec replied in unison, 'You're *sssssssooooooooooo* sexy!' It was a fun start to an extraordinary night that was watched by nearly fourteen million viewers. The atmosphere was electric and the studio was packed full of fans cheering on their favourite finalist. As Young sang his first song of the night, Cowell revised his prediction of who would win and became convinced Young would beat his favourite, Gates. As a result, he felt miserable.

Young and Gates performed both of the songs on the winner's single, and each reprised a song from earlier in the series. In Young's case it was 'Light My Fire'; in Gates's, 'Unchained Melody'. At this point, the judges expressed support for both singers, but Cowell's disappointment at Young's apparent upper hand continued to rankle.

When asked to sum up the series, though, Cowell described it as 'the best six months of my life'. Could a Gates victory put the icing on the cake for Cowell? He waited backstage between the main show and the results. There were celebrities galore backstage, including comedian Ricky Gervais, Lisa from Steps and actress Tamzin Outhwaite, all passionately discussing the performances and who they thought would win. Members of the production team ran around excitedly, coming into Cowell's dressing room to tell him the latest news from the public vote. The lead changed regularly and it was clearly going to be a tight finish.

Finally, Cowell got a call to return to the studio for the results. He was now minutes away from discovering who had won. Was it Young, or had his favourite, Gates, grabbed the title? He knew that nine million votes had been cast, so whoever won was going to have a huge thumbs-up for their future career. Cowell tried to find out who had won before the show went on air, but none of the production team would let him know – they told him to wait and hear it along with the rest of the nation. He watched the floor manager like a hawk, knowing that he was about to be told the results into his headphones. The floor manager stopped dead and said, 'You're kidding?' into his mouthpiece. Cowell asked him who had won and the floor manager discreetly mouthed 'Will'. He was bitterly disappointed and admits that he faked his smile when the result was officially announced. Confirmed as the winner, Young then sang 'Evergreen'. 'There you go,' said Ant, 'that's it, that's the end of *Pop Idol* 2002.'

Cowell returned backstage and, along with Fuller, tried to console Gates, who was extremely disappointed and upset at not winning. Cowell was seen on camera congratulating Young backstage. 'Well done,' he said rather coolly, 'you deserved it on the night.' It was a less than passionately delivered sentiment. Just as he had been honest – at times brutal – with contestants in his feedback, so he was very upfront about where his loyalties lay on the night. He had wanted Gates to win and he didn't hide his disappointment. Not that this meant Cowell would not be giving Young his full professional support as his career was launched. Indeed, in the days and weeks that followed, Cowell concluded that he had in Young a very good performer and a very gentlemanly character. A profitable one too: Young's winners' single went straight to number one, selling 1.1 million copies in the first week it was on sale. When Young visited the BMG offices, noted Cowell, the reaction of the staff was one of genuine excitement among people not unfamiliar with first-hand encounters with famous faces.

Ultimately, Cowell decided that due to his and Young's history of conflict on *Pop Idol* and his vocal backing of Gates, he would have to allow other BMG luminaries to work with Young. 'I never hit it off with Will Young,' he later revealed. 'I blame myself for not being able to work with him. I lashed out, which was the wrong thing to do. I don't think he'd want to work with me in a million years, which is a shame because I rate him as an artist. Will is better than Gareth – there's no doubt about that in my mind – but Gareth was the pop idol. And at the end of the day, both of them have done bloody well.'

Cleverly, despite his disappointment at Young's victory, Cowell managed to have his cake and eat it, as he also launched the career of his beloved Gates. The singer recorded 'Unchained Melody' and flew to Florida to record the video. When he first performed the song on *Pop Idol*, Cowell told Gates that he would get a number one with it. His prediction proved spot-on, as the single went on to sell 950,000 copies in the first week and did indeed take the top spot in the charts. The single ultimately sold 1.5 million copies. Not as high a number as the same single by Robson and Jerome, but still a mammoth achievement.

Cowell had managed to launch not one, but two pop idols in the wake of the show, and he even tried to sign Darius Danesh. He arranged to meet Danesh at the BMG offices, but a power cut in the area meant the pair reconvened at Cowell's flat in Holland Park. The flat, recalled Danesh in his book, was a true bachelor pad. The rooms were sparsely furnished and it had marble floors. It certainly didn't feel lived in, he thought. Cowell explained that he had designed it for 'ultimate convenience', but Danesh found it reminiscent of the legal drama flick *The Devil's Advocate*.

The Scot came under intense pressure to go along with what Cowell wanted, which was for Danesh to launch his solo career with a cover of 'You've Lost That Lovin' Feeling'. This wasn't what Danesh had in mind. He played Cowell some songs that he had written, but he got short shrift. In the end, Danesh walked away from what Cowell and Waterman offered and managed to free himself from the tight contractual obligations that all *Pop Idol* finalists were under. When he bumped into Cowell months later at a charity auction, Cowell assured him there were no hard feelings. 'No lovey, no darling,' said Cowell, and walked off chuckling.

There is a postscript to the story of Cowell's relationship with Danesh. When Danesh's self-penned debut single 'Colourblind' came fourth in the vote for Record of the Year, he received a cheeky phone call from Cowell. What was it like losing again tonight, asked Cowell. Once more, Danesh had the perfect riposte, pointing out that his was the only original song in the top five, which was otherwise composed of cover versions. 'So I'm actually going out celebrating tonight,' he told Cowell. 'What are you doing?' Just as he had silenced Cowell with his 'loosen your belt' quip on *Pop Idol*, so he once more got the better of him. Cowell must have been relieved that not all contestants were as sharp-witted as Danesh. In due course he would refine his patter so he didn't leave the door wide open for attack. Although Danesh enjoyed his own path, Cowell insists that under his guidance Danesh would have been more of a success.

Due to his blunt, straight-talking demeanour as a *Pop Idol* judge, during the broadcast of the show Cowell became something of a hate figure for viewers. He received lots of hate mail, though he insists that only one out of every ten letters he received was abusive, and he claims not to have taken the tag Mr Nasty seriously. All the same, he was enjoying his new-found infamy and believed he could turn it to his advantage professionally. 'Personally, my friends think it's just fun, so it doesn't make any difference there,' he said in the *Pop Idol* book. 'Professionally, I think it's going to help because if you are well known for speaking your mind, hopefully when you find people with an extra talent they'll like the idea of being signed by you.'

Cowell's reputation as the tough-talking, honest man of music was secure and also to his advantage. However, straight talk wasn't the only thing he became known for as a result of his *Pop Idol* exposure. Another thing he had become celebrated for at this stage were his trousers. During the making of *Pop Idol*, several people had noticed that Cowell wore very high-waisted trousers, and with his jumpers tucked in, it gave him a very distinctive look. It had once been fashionable for men to wear their trousers this way, but that time was firmly in the past. Naturally, in a show full of banter, Cowell's sartorial tastes were going to be remarked upon. Presenters Ant and Dec regularly mocked him for his trousers, during the amusing sketches in which they dressed up as the judges.

During one show, Dec dressed up as Cowell, complete with high-waisted trousers. Ant jokingly told him he'd left his flies undone. 'Oh no,' sighed Dec. 'You don't mean you can see my… nipples?!' Cowell laughed along with them, but admitted to being baffled at first. He had always worn his trousers that way and nobody had ever commented on it. However, having appeared on *Pop Idol*, he encountered remarks wherever he went, and when he was introduced to people, he started to notice their eyes moving down to his waist. He wasn't the only judge to take a bit of flack for his taste in clothes; Neil Fox got hammered in the press for wearing a loud pink shirt during one episode. He held up his hands and quickly changed his ways. 'It looked awful and I got a lot of stick in the press – deservedly – and enough flack from the other judges,' he told the official *Pop Idol* book. 'I've always been a loud-shirt man, but sitting there on an important TV show, that wouldn't be the right thing to wear.'

Cowell too was quick to grasp the outcome of wearing distinctive clothes on national television. It's no exaggeration to say that Cowell's trousers really captured the public's imagination and they soon became a national obsession. Writing in the *Star*, showbiz correspondent Gary Bushell named Cowell's trousers as the top talking point of 2002, while over at the *Sun*, Dominic Mohan included a question about them in his end-of-year quiz. Who, he asked his readers, is the 'Mr Nasty whose nipple-high trousers became his trademark?' Meanwhile, up in Scotland, a *Daily Record* journalist described Cowell as, 'An odd Popeye shape, thanks to his high-waisted trousers.' It wasn't only journalists who discussed the style of his legwear in the pages of the tabloid press. One Mirror reader, Naela Shakir, wrote in to defend them, however, writing, 'Simon Cowell's high-waist trousers rock!'

Her supportive stance was rare, though. There was far too much fun to be had by taking the mickey out of the man who made a living out of being critical of others – including their dress sense – on national TV. Having dished it out, Cowell was learning to take a lot back. Fenwick's department store in Newcastle soon joined in with the fun. The store designers put together an alternative nativity scene in their window for Christmas 2002. The theme was a collection of things an alien would take back to his planet from Earth. Included were a snowman in a fridge, football star David Beckham's mohican and Cowell's high-waisted trousers.

Still, there was no respite for poor Cowell. The *Sun* declared that the question on everyone's lips was, 'Do his high-waisted trousers have an agent all of their own yet?' The trousers might not have had official representation, but as we have seen, Cowell himself had a press agent in the form of Max Clifford. However, even Clifford couldn't resist joining in when it came to mocking his client's trousers. He told reporters he was planning to take Cowell to see a new extreme ride at Blackpool Pleasure Beach. 'It'll lift his trousers even higher,' he laughed. Cowell claims he found all the banter 'hilarious'. It's lucky he has a good sense of humour; he would need it as the fun continued at his expense.

The *Sun* found a problem with the posters for a new James Bond film, saying his high-waisted trousers made Pierce Brosnan look like Cowell. The broadsheets were at it, too. Writing style tips in *The Independent*, Clare Dwyer Hogg said, 'An obvious example of how not to wear [trousers] is Simon Cowell, with his spectacularly high-waisted pair.' A political report in the same newspaper even used Cowell's trousers as a reference point. When Andy McSmith followed Tony Blair around Basra in Iraq, he observed, 'While his shirt looked wrinkle-free and damp-free by the end of the day, his high-waisted, dark blue trousers would have made Simon Cowell blush.' Over in *The Guardian*, *GQ* magazine editor Dylan Jones wrote about how he embarked on a *Pop Idol*-style search for new fashion models. 'Speaking to people back in London, they all ask if I'm the "new" Simon Cowell,' he wrote. 'Am I being rude to people? Am I belting my trousers just below my nipples?' Cowell could at least console himself that *The Guardian* and *The Daily Telegraph* both ran features saying that he had brought high-waisted trousers back into fashion. It wasn't as if Cowell was shy of criticizing the dress sense of other people, either. Of *Pop Idol* producer Nigel Lythgoe, he said, 'He must have been sponsored by C&A, who closed down shortly afterwards, of course.'

Not that this took the heat off him. When Cowell invited a *News of the World* journalist to his home for an interview, the reporter insisted on viewing his wardrobe and duly reported that there was a row of twenty or more of the famous trousers. After being mocked for his dress sense for over a year, Cowell admitted during the interview that he was going to change his style. 'I wear the jumpers untucked now,' he said. 'Do you blame me? Wouldn't you if you were me and had had the press I had? It wasn't a conscious thing about changing an image as such, but I must admit I did get embarrassed.' When Madame Tussauds commissioned a waxwork model of Cowell, he reportedly insisted that the model should not wear high-waisted trousers. In the end, he shrugged off the embarrassment and went along with the fun as best he could. He duly donated a pair of his trousers to a *Heat* magazine auction for the charity Crusaid. Asked whether he would be bidding on any items, *Heat* magazine editor Mark Frith said, 'Well, I'm very tempted by Simon Cowell's trousers. He's donating his high trousers. I don't know if the belt is included but I hope it is.'

Although he has dropped the high-waisted-trouser look and moved on, Cowell is still haunted by his strides to this day. He had learned a very important lesson about life in the public eye. He wouldn't give people the opportunity to mock him so easily in future. That said, the trouser-teasing continues. In March 2009 a journalist writing about Cowell's shopping habits in *The Independent* speculated that when he buys trousers, Cowell has to give the store assistant his chest size rather than his waist size.

A new wardrobe wasn't the only change in the air for Cowell at this time; he also consulted a life coach. He first met Donna Aston in 2000. Then aged thirty-four, she was Australia's top health and fitness expert, and a former contestant on Miss Australia. She went on to give Cowell some dietary and lifestyle tips and turned his fortunes around. 'I'm a new man and feel a lot better for it. Donna has made me a nicer Mr Nasty,' he claimed. 'I used to miss out on fruit and veg, but Donna's changed all that and taught me to cut down on things like bread and preservatives. I now have fixed meal times and am sleeping better. It's helped me cope with all the stress of a very hectic six months and I don't get irritated so often.' A lack of irritability – would this lead to a new Simon Cowell who delivered fewer put-downs in the future? He wasn't saying, but he did reveal that Aston never gave him a Cowell-style verdict. 'That's probably why our relationship has worked so well,' he joked. 'She doesn't put me down. She must realize I can't take it, I can only give it out. Donna helped me focus my mind – she didn't criticize me, but she made me realize I was eating loads of junk.'

Aston confirmed that Cowell's eating habits and lifestyle were making him feeling run down. 'He was eating loads of convenience food because he was so busy, but he was depriving himself of a lot of nutrition that his body really needed,' she said. 'Simon wasn't in particularly bad shape – his biggest goal was just to feel better. His main issue was that he had a busy schedule with *Pop Idol*. He wanted to make sure he could keep up with it and have the energy and endurance without running himself into the ground.' Cowell insisted that he wasn't about to turn evangelical about his new lifestyle, at least not with his *Pop Idol* colleagues. 'I haven't shared my secret with the other judges though. Trying to get Peter Waterman to give up sausages after fifty years would just be too hard!' What with Waterman joking about Cowell's trousers in *The Observer* and Cowell returning the compliment in the *News of the World*, the first series might be over, but the banter between the judges and old friends continued.

Another significant relationship in Cowell's life began at this point – with a stunningly beautiful model called Terri Seymour. He had first met Seymour in the early 1990s, when she was eighteen. The best part of a decade later, they met again when she interviewed Cowell for a television show in LA, and in the wake of the interview they began dating. Seymour, fifteen years younger than Cowell, was raised by her mother and never knew her father. In the early days of their relationship, it was reported that things were rather volatile between the pair, and Cowell has described her as having a fiery temper. However, before long things were going so well that she moved into Cowell's plush Holland Park home. For a character like Cowell, this was a big step. Friends who he had previously relied on noted that his relationship with Seymour made him a more self-sufficient character. Naturally, the press took great interest in Cowell's relationship with this glamorous younger lady. 'To me, relationships are a bit like work,' he told the

*Daily Mail.* 'When the buzz has gone and it fizzles out, then it's time to move on. Things are cool at the moment with Terri, but who knows how she will feel next week, or next month?'

The next question Cowell had to ponder was whether he wanted to appear in a second series of *Pop Idol.* Despite having enjoyed the experience of the first series, calling it the best time of his life, Cowell was far from enthusiastic about the prospect of going through it all again. After mulling it over, however, he signed up for the second series in March 2003. It was clear from the start that the second series of *Pop Idol* had a lot to live up to. The first series had been a mammoth success, and anticipation for series two was high, with 20,000 people applying to take part, twice the number of applicants as for the first series. Apart from a few tweaks, the basic format remained the same, as did the judging panel and presenters. However, for many people things just weren't the same the second time round. With contestants savvy about what to expect, much of the tension was removed. When Cowell delivered his verdicts in series one, the shock the contestants felt at his bluntness made for gripping viewing, but the second time round, everyone knew what to expect. Furthermore, having seen the success that Will Young enjoyed in the wake of his retort to Cowell, many of the series two contestants tried to repeat the trick with comebacks of their own. However, where Young had seemed charming and spontaneous when he answered back, in series two those who fought back often came across as contrived and obnoxious. Some even arrived with confrontation openly in their sights: 'Simon Cowell,' said one contestant defiantly just before entering the audition room, 'I'm coming to get you, brother!'

Even on the first day of filming, Cowell was concerned about how series two would pan out. Since the first series, he and his fellow judges had become celebrities in their own right. Consequently, he was concerned about becoming a parody of himself, playing up to the cameras by offering ever more withering assessments of the auditionees' performances. This was easier said than done on the opening day, when he was taken aback by how many poor singers auditioned. It seemed that Cowell's bluntness hadn't put off average (or worse) performers; far from it, there were even more the second time round. Cowell noted that some auditionees were well aware of the fact that they couldn't sing and were simply having a laugh at the show's expense. There were some genuinely deluded bad singers, but inevitably the show attracted plenty of applicants who were essentially there to pull a practical joke and get on the television. Cowell was usually the first of the judges to identify such pranksters. When a man arrived wearing a top hat and banana outfit to sing 'I've Got You Under My Skin', Cowell asked him to hold out his top hat. He put a five pound note in it and said, 'That's saved you an hour outside a tube station, off you go.'

One auditionee who stood out quickly for all the wrong reasons was Warren Wald, a maths graduate. He sang 'Eye of the Tiger', the 1980s hit song from the movie *Rocky*. It was a poor performance, and a comical one. Chapman and Fox giggled, while Waterman looked horrified. As for Cowell, he seemed genuinely stunned by the lack of quality in Wald's rendition. At the end of the performance Fox was sobbing with laughter. 'Not the reaction I had expected,' confessed the singer. After the other judges had their say, Cowell said, 'I don't think anyone in London is as bad as you – and London's a big city.' Wald seemed genuinely shocked by the poor feedback he received. As he was about to leave, Cowell added, 'Warren, one bit of advice. If you've got a maths degree, stick with the mathematics. Off you go, bye.' Off he went... to become one of the more famous people to emerge from the series. After the episode was broadcast, the British public took to Wald in an Eddie-the-Eagle way, and he was featured in newspapers and television shows.

A female contestant claimed that she saw Cowell and his girlfriend Seymour sneak off for a bit of nookie during filming. 'It was the biggest piece of gossip we had all week,' Laura McGavigan told the *Daily Star*. 'His zip was open and there was no question what he and his girlfriend had been up to. I had watched them whisper to each other, sneak off and then return with such a look of guilt. They really didn't think anyone had seen them. It doesn't take half an hour to go to the loo, does it? The toilets were in the other direction anyway.' She continued, 'It was *so* funny. We saw Simon and his girlfriend disappear together and then he came back thirty minutes later. Loads of people saw him return and we all started sniggering because his flies were wide open. They were still all over each other as they reappeared, looking very lovey-dovey and satisfied. We tried hard not to laugh too much, but it was obvious what he'd been up to. They both looked very flushed and coy. He's very naughty.'

Cowell was in a generally naughty mood in series two, as the bad singers soon discovered. Throughout the early auditions, Cowell was unsparing in his comments. 'I don't think you know how bad you sound, no seriously,' he told a contestant called Emily, after she'd murdered 'Don't Cry For Me Argentina'. Later, a male singer with a high-pitched voice auditioned, and Cowell dispatched him with a simple, 'I think you're the worst we have ever heard.' If Emily had been somewhat nasal, then a young lady called Hayley surpassed herself with a performance of 'Sometimes' by Britney Spears, which she delivered almost entirely through her nose. Cowell creased up laughing throughout the performance, covering up his face in an attempt to control his hysterics. Having composed himself when she finished, he asked her, 'You're not serious about this?' She said she was. 'Don't,' he replied, simply, and sent her on her way. When Leon McPherson auditioned, Cowell told him, 'You sounded like a warped record.' A female contestant who sang 'The Power of Love' was disappointed to be told, 'That song does one of two things: it either transfixes you because it's a beautiful love song, or it sends you to sleep. And you fell into the latter – we've had the musical version of Valium.' Another was dispatched with, 'Your voice isn't even good enough for a cruise ship.'

As the auditions continued, Cowell faced more contestants 'doing a Will' and answering back. One such person was nineteen-year-old Daniel Webster, who proved to be one of series two's more controversial figures. He turned up looking mildly eccentric, with a loud blond quiff and wearing a glittery gold jacket with matching glittery bow tie. He told Ant and Dec that he knew a lot about the judges, including where they lived. In the audition room, he announced he was going to sing Soft Cell's 'Tainted Love'. 'I heard you were doing it on the dinner table last night,' he told the stunned panel. Chapman asked how he learned of this. 'I know a lot about people,' he continued eerily. Pointing at Cowell, he said, 'I know you've got a million-pound house in Holland Park.' He then disclosed other facts he knew about the panel. 'I know a lot about people,' he repeated, then he sang 'Tainted Love'. At the song's conclusion, Cowell told him, 'Daniel, you are one of the worst singers I have heard in my entire life. You were diabolical – crap.' Webster shot back straight away, 'Yeah, but you think everyone's terrible.' While Waterman and Chapman burst out laughing at Webster's retort, Cowell was not amused and sent the singer packing. When he watched the broadcasts later, Webster was very unhappy with the way the show portrayed him. As he later said to the *Sun*, he felt they'd made him look like a stalker.

Cowell faced allegations of nepotism when Gareth Gates's sister Nicola arrived to audition for the second series running. Where her brother had sailed all the way to the final in series one, Nicola had been eliminated at the first hurdle, when Cowell told her she was short of confidence and needed a vocal coach. She returned for series two and it seemed that this time round she had too much confidence. She arrived at the Manchester auditions with a new look, a new name, 'Nicola J' (her middle name is Jayne), and something of an attitude. Her performance didn't impress most of the judges, but Cowell put her through, admitting he was doing so because of her connection with Gates. Fox stormed, 'Doesn't that strike you as unbelievably unfair?' She was eliminated at the next phase of the competition, with Waterman telling her she was following in a giant's footsteps. It seemed that the shadow of Cowell's favouritism towards Gareth Gates in the first series was going to be cast over series two.

There were plenty of singers who disappointed the panel for different reasons. However, as they toured the UK during three weeks of auditions, Cowell and his fellow judges noticed that there were also plenty of talented singers turning up. Among these was a large girl who auditioned in Glasgow. Michelle McManus was described by Cowell as 'a big girl with a large voice'. When she arrived to audition, she raised eyebrows because of her large physique. Chapman asked her why she had come to audition. 'Because I want this,' said McManus, with determination in her voice. 'I'm going to do this.' Chapman was impressed. 'Good girl,' she told her. McManus explained that she was going to sing Celine Dion's, 'Because You Love Me'. 'One of my favourite songs of all time,' said Cowell. 'I love it.' In time, he would go on to express love for McManus, too.

At the end of her performance, Chapman told McManus, 'You're one of the better singers I have seen today. We've seen some terrible singers, but we've also seen some good ones. I'm going to say a definite yes to you.' In series one, Waterman had railed against the progression of another fat contestant, Rik Waller, so it was no surprise when he told McManus, 'I think you are not a pop idol, you'll never be a pop idol, but that doesn't mean you're not a great singer.' Cowell said, 'I'm going to say yes.' With Fox absent from this audition, McManus's progression to the next round was sealed. 'Thank you so much,' she said, looking emotional. 'I *will* do this.' Her determination was palpable, her words prescient. Cowell insists that, thanks to the likes of McManus, the second series of *Pop Idol* was more interesting for him and produced better entertainment for viewers. He felt the second series was much more about talent, rather than image. He enjoyed the diversity of the contestants, and later wrote that he was 'sick to death of seeing wave after wave of Atomic Kitten clones'. Another singer who bucked the image trend was Kimberley, a mother of two with a fuller figure.

A very talented and memorable contestant from series two was Susanne Manning, who sang 'Killing Me Softly' at her first audition. With a geeky, slightly awkward air, she nonetheless oozed beauty, charisma and talent from the start and sang the song beautifully. Fox and Chapman both praised her performance and voted for her to go through, with Fox telling her, 'You have lips every man wants to kiss, you've got a great voice.' Chapman was also positive, but Waterman disagreed with their praise. He said her aspirations were a 'crazy dream' and voted 'no', saying, 'It was an uninspired vocal, ordinary, just lifeless.' When it came to Cowell's turn, he disagreed with Waterman and his vote put her through to the next stage. He has since said that he really liked her, but was concerned from the start that her shyness would work against her. Nevertheless, he gave her great feedback and she went through to the next round.

Manning – now married and known as Susanne Courtney – says it was always Cowell's approval she most hoped for. 'I'd watched series one and I'd sit with my mates and say "She was rubbish, he's really good" and so on,' she says, relaxing in the canteen at BBC Radio Berkshire, where she now works as a co-presenter and producer. 'I always had an opinion and my opinion was always the same as Simon's. Even when he was rude I'd say, "But he's right!"' Soon, her friends were encouraging her to apply for the second series of the show, and that's how she found herself standing in front of the judging panel at the London auditions. Courtney was understandably nervous, particularly about Cowell's verdict. 'I didn't know whether I was a good singer or not,' she says. 'Nobody in my family is musical. Friends used to tell me I could sing, but I'm quite a pessimist so I didn't necessarily believe them. I thought, These people have never met me, they don't know me, they don't need to say nice things.' I knew that Simon would give it to me straight. He was the one whose praise you wanted more than any judge. He probably still is [on *The X Factor* and other shows], but I'm not quite so sure he's as from the gut as he used to be.'

Courtney explains that much as Cowell would dish out criticism during filming, he didn't have a harsh persona when it came to his off-screen dealings. 'We didn't have much contact with the judges off camera because our schedules for the live shows rarely crossed over,' she says. 'I remember once, though, when we finalists were recording a video for the Christmas single. Simon had really slagged me off just two days before on the show, using the words "train wreck" and "hideous" to describe my performance of "I Guess That's Why They Call It The Blues". But at the video shoot he breezed up to me as if none of that had happened and gave me a huge bear hug! In my head I thought, I don't know what to do with this man. I don't know what to say!' So she simply returned the embrace. Soon enough, she recalls, he retracted his harsh words. 'To be fair to him, the next week he apologized and said that after listening back to it, he'd realized it wasn't as bad as he'd said. That was really nice.' Nowadays, Courtney recalls her brush with *Pop Idol* and Cowell as 'a cool footnote' in her life.

Manning was not the only contestant that Cowell and Waterman disagreed over during the opening auditions. Their row over Danesh in series one had made for memorable television, and there were further disagreements in series two. One singer that sparked flames between them was Sam Nixon from Barnsley. A short, good-looking boy with a rocky image, he drew praise from

Cowell at his first audition, who told him, 'You're one of the best – that's what we're looking for.' Cowell then asked Waterman to add his opinion. 'Speechless,' sighed Waterman. 'You didn't like it?' asked Cowell. 'No, not at all,' replied his fellow judge. Cowell asked if he was winding him up. 'No, you're winding *me* up,' said Waterman as Nixon looked on anxiously. Nonetheless, he was voted through by the panel.

There were further sparks when Andy Scott-Lee arrived. Scott-Lee had been a member of a boyband called 3SL and was the brother of Steps singer Lisa Scott-Lee. Waterman was keen to avoid allegations of nepotism in his comments and verdict, due to his connection with Steps, and therefore declined to comment at first on Scott-Lee's performance. 'I'm going to completely abstain because Lisa is a friend of mine, so I'm not sure whether I want to be part of this,' he said. Cowell leapt on this. 'That's the coward's way out,' he said. 'You're patronizing him.' The accusation sparked a repetitive, heated exchange between the two judges.

Waterman: 'No I'm not.'

Cowell: 'Yes you are.'

Waterman: 'No I'm not.'

Cowell: 'Yes you are.'

Waterman: 'No I'm not.'

Cowell: 'Yes you are.'

Waterman: 'No I'm not.'

Cowell: '*Yes* you are.'

Cowell had a twinkle in his eye throughout the exchange. He clearly enjoyed their squabbles and knew that they made for great television. Fox interrupted the pair saying, 'This isn't pantomime – yes or no?' Waterman eventually relented and offered a verdict. He voted to put Scott-Lee through. As the relieved singer left the room, Waterman whacked Cowell with a pile of paper and the panel laughed off the whole exchange. 'Look at you two,' sighed Fox.

A singer in the opening round who prompted some amusing reactions from Cowell was Scouse bingo-caller Rachel Iyfon, who was loud and full of beans. When she arrived at the audition, Fox asked her where she was from. 'This is a hard one to explain,' began the bubbly, loquacious singer. 'I was born in Liverpool, moved over to Birkenhead, moved back to Liverpool, then I moved back to Birkenhead with my sister.' Cowell summed up: 'Right, so you're from Birkenhead.' Although he gave her short shrift about her singing, Cowell was clearly fond of the hyperactive, chatty and slighty crazy singer. As she consistently interrupted the judges during their verdicts, he stepped in: 'OK, just for one moment, pause,' he said with a growing smile on his face. 'I *do* like you, you're very funny.' She interrupted and asked for more advice. Cowell's advice was simple, 'Shut up!' He says he found her, 'absolutely hysterical' and that if the show was *Personality Idol* he would make her the winner on the spot. As it was, she was sent through to the next round.

And so the first round of auditions came to an end.

As in series one, the next phase of the competition was held at the Criterion Theatre in London, where the final one hundred contestants would be whittled down to a final fifty, who could go on to face the public vote during the next round at Teddington Studios. The last time round at the Criterion, Cowell had argued with Waterman about overweight contestant Rik Waller.

This time, they argued about another large contender, McManus. 'I think she should stay in,' said Cowell. 'What, as the Weather Girls?' asked Waterman. Chapman agreed with Cowell that McManus should progress, but Fox sided with Waterman. 'She hasn't got an image,' added Waterman. They then discussed another large contestant, Kimberley. Cowell asked Waterman what he thought of her. 'I think this has become a bloody joke, personally,' he scoffed. Cowell asked where the harm was in putting her and McManus through. 'How many people like that in the past forty years have you seen sell a million records?' asked Waterman. 'How many people like Will Young have you seen?' countered Cowell with a cheeky smile on his face. He could see another row brewing and was obviously loving it. Waterman repeated his question. 'Mama Cass, Alison Moyet, Meatloaf,' listed Cowell. 'That'll do, I'll take them.'

The pair also argued bitterly about a contestant called Tarek, who was something of an eccentric. He wasn't a particularly talented singer, but he oozed personality, even if he was a bit irritating at times. 'Pete threw a fit again,' wrote Cowell in *I Don't Mean to Be Rude, But...* 'That's why I am so fond of Pete. He speaks his mind and doesn't give a shit.' Again, Cowell emerged triumphant from the disagreement. In the end, both McManus and Kimberley got put through, as did Tarek. However, Cowell was keen to placate his fuming friend. 'Has Mr Grumpy gone?' he asked of Waterman, who replied that he thought Cowell was 'crazy'. It was a disagreement that would reappear during the series, particularly at the end of the final.

Once more, the contestants were called to the stage in groups and given either the good or bad news. When it came to McManus's group, the tension was electric. She was already proving to be a contestant who polarized opinion. What did it mean to be in her group? Having toyed with them a bit, Cowell smiled and told them they were through, ensuring pandemonium and joy on the stage. As the triumphant group left the stage, McManus poignantly stopped, looked at Cowell and emotionally mouthed, 'Thank you.' He nodded and smiled back. A rapport had clearly developed between him and McManus. The Scot was in the first group of ten to face the public vote at Teddington Studios. Cowell said after her performance, 'I think you're going to breeze through this round and make the top ten, and I want you in the top ten because I think you're great.' As she clearly filled up with emotion, Cowell added, 'Just be yourself.' As she left the stage, he gave her an encouraging wink. It was the first time we'd seen the Cowell wink, which has gone on to become a legendary part of the shows he judges, including *The X Factor* and *Britain's Got Talent*.

Cowell's encouragement of McManus – which was to grow during the live finals – was richly significant for two reasons. Most importantly it showed the public his sweeter side. In series one he had become known mostly for his blunt honesty. He was 'Mr Nasty' and rarely showed that he is actually a caring man with a surprisingly big heart. True, he was supportive of Gates in the first series, but that came across as commercial support. It was as if he could see the pound signs flashing in front of his eyes when he saw Gates perform, and was roaring him on for that reason alone. However, by supporting McManus he was, in many ways, backing the underdog. For whatever reason – perhaps because he felt there was no natural winner in series two – he became as partisan towards her as he had been with Gates. But this time there was a mentoring edge to his encouragement.

Which brings us to the other significant aspect of his relationship with McManus. By becoming her de facto mentor, he was going above and beyond his prescribed role as a judge. There was nothing in the rules of the show that prevented him from having a favourite, but by vocally encouraging one contestant over the others, he added a new dimension and dynamic to the competition. Could it be that it was here, as he took McManus under his wing, that Cowell realized that judges mentoring individual contestants during the latter stages of the competition made for a winning formula? She was voted through from the first week of the final-fifty rounds, so Cowell had his wish of McManus being in the top ten. Now, they had four more weeks before the live shows commenced.

Cowell continued to entertain with his comments at the Teddington Studios. When Roxanne Cooper sang 'Beautiful' she was told she was 'excellent' by Waterman. Cowell pulled a serious expression and said, 'I disagree with Pete, I don't think that was excellent.' Cooper's face dropped until Cowell added, 'I thought it was *sensational*!' Her relief was overwhelming. Not that the entertainment Cowell provided always had a happy ending. 'When you sing, you remind me of a cod on a fisherman's slab,' he told one female contestant, much to her chagrin. 'Your eyes – they are totally and utterly dead.' Then, when Tarek murdered a Robbie Williams number, Cowell sighed, 'Oh Tarek, what was the song called?' 'Let Me Entertain You,' Tarek replied. 'My answer is – no.' When he was critiquing the performance of Scottish Craig Chalmers, the contestant protested, 'I've worked very hard for this competition, everybody knows that.' Cowell was having none of it, though. '*Everyone* has,' he corrected Chalmers. The Scot disagreed, '*Some* people have worked hard.' Cowell interrupted again, 'No, you've *all* worked hard – let's establish that.' Chalmers, previously a favourite to make the final ten, was voted out following his exchange with Cowell, though he has since reappeared on another reality show, BBC1's *Any Dream Will Do*.

When the final-fifty round was complete, a change in the format was introduced with a wildcard round, so that some of the better performers who hadn't been voted through could have a second chance. This round saw Manning and Nixon return to the running; the final twelve were now ready to perform in the live finals. For Cowell, it was all about McManus most weeks, although in the first round of the live shows, McManus, who had been ill, sang 'All By Myself' and faced criticism from Cowell. He told her she'd 'have to do a lot better than that to stay in this competition'. This, though, was caring advice rather than a putdown. McManus took it as such and was voted through.

As the live shows progressed, the feeling that the finalists in series two were not as talented and charismatic as those in series one was hard to avoid. Instead, the real star of the show was Cowell. Week after week, his feedback was memorable. He told Marc Dillon, 'Someone else is going to come out and blow everyone away and you will be forgotten about.' Dillon, presumably attempting 'a Will', answered, 'That's fine, it's not a problem at all.' Cowell calmly shot straight back, 'Well, it is a problem.' Dillon shrugged. 'Well, for *you*.' Cowell had the last word, though: 'No,' he told Dillon. 'Not for me – for you.' Sure enough, Dillon was voted off by the public that week. The days of Young, Gates and Danesh seemed a million miles away as another forgettable contestant left the show with more of a whimper than a bang.

The other main drama revolved round the progress of McManus, who continued to defy pop stereotypes by being voted through week after week in spite of her large figure. The week after Dillon's departure, Cowell's love of McManus grew and was formally declared for the first time. 'Forget the fact that I'm in the record business,' he told her after her performance, 'as a fan: I *love* you.' She smiled and bowed, replying, 'I love you too! I love you too!' The same week, Cowell told Scott-Lee that he was 'mediocre', prompting a disagreement from Waterman. 'He ain't mediocre,' he told Cowell, who replied, 'Pete, one of the signs of old age is that you start to lose your hearing.' Waterman replied, 'Pardon?' Cowell rolled his eyes and said, 'Exactly.' Later, in the same show, Cowell managed an indirect pop at his series-one nemesis Will Young. Sam Nixon had sung 'Blame it on the Boogie', which as Cowell reminded viewers was the song Young performed at his first, forgettable audition on series one. 'He's kept very quiet about it,' quipped Cowell. There was just time for one more Cowell/McManus love-in – 'I can't imagine the final without you, so I hope they vote you through,' he told her – and the evening's show was complete.

The final two were Cowell's favourite McManus and Brummie boy Mark Rhodes. It was the final two the public had chosen – there was shock when favourite Nixon was voted out in the semi-finals – but the pair lacked the dynamism of Young and Gates. Once again, the week before the final, McManus and Rhodes undertook an election-style campaign to win more votes, complete with battle buses. However, compared with the final week of series one, where Will- and Garethmania swept the nation, it was a relatively low-key affair. The only edge that was lent to the week was by a running practical joke McManus played on Rhodes. She arranged that everywhere he went, he was handed a block of cheese, in reference to a regular criticism from Fox that Rhodes was a cheesy performer. It might have seemed harmless banter, but it left Rhodes in a quandary about how to answer back. He could hardly mock McManus for her most obvious characteristic – her weight.

On the night of the final, both singers performed what was to be the winners' single, 'All This Time'. Each was given a separate B-side to sing and each reprised a favourite performance from earlier in the series. Rhodes chose 'She's Like the Wind', while McManus opted for 'On My Radio'. Cowell was supportive of McManus all evening, telling her, 'I'm very proud that you're here, Michelle. Good for you.' In choosing the word 'proud', Cowell once more revealed his personal stake in her success and the fact that he obviously saw himself as her mentor. At the end of the evening, Ant and Dec called both contestants to the stage to reveal who had won. Over 10.26 million votes had been cast, they said (over a million more than were cast in the final of series one) and then announced, to Cowell's enormous delight, that the winner was McManus. The Scot was hugely emotional on hearing the news. She had taken a lot of flack for her weight, and choked back the tears as she said, 'I just want to say for everyone who said I couldn't do it, well, I've done it.' Cowell applauded wildly, but one of his fellow judges was less than happy.

As Cowell cheered at the result, off-camera Waterman stormed off the set angrily. He had opposed McManus's progress throughout the competition. From her first audition, when he told her, 'You will never be a pop idol,' through to his row with Cowell at the Criterion Theatre and beyond, he had felt that despite her good voice, she had the wrong image for the pop industry. He told McManus she had 'zero personality and zero charisma'. Furious at her victory, he declared the result a 'travesty' and stormed out of the studio, reportedly refusing to attend the after-show party to celebrate her success. It was a bitter end to a series that had failed to live up to the glory of its predecessor. Waterman vowed never to judge another reality show again, and in the aftermath of the final, he slammed McManus in the press. 'She won't even last six months,' he said, branding McManus 'rubbish'. He also turned on Cowell, saying of his support for the Scot, 'He had an agenda. He wanted Michelle to win and she did. Will Young was a fantastic winner, Michelle is not.' Fox defended the winner, saying, 'Pete has behaved like a prat. I wish he'd shut up and be happy for Michelle. She's got a great voice.'

The victory for Cowell's favourite contestant proved controversial. Writing in the *Mirror*, columnist Tony Parsons argued that her victory was a 'triumph for political correctness'. Parsons complained, 'Nobody had the nerve to come out and state the obvious – sorry, but there's no way a woman, never mind a popstar, that young should be that fat.' However, for Cowell her victory was a triumph. Journalist Jenni Murray wrote in *The Independent* that Cowell had previously admitted to her that in the second series of *Pop Idol*, the show was hoping to find someone 'a bit different'. Well, in the shape of McManus they had succeeded. At the forefront of McManus's *Pop Idol* victory had been Cowell's vocal support for her, and he had done no harm at all to his own reputation by backing a candidate with such an unconventional image. The runner-up Rhodes was not a singer who Cowell had ever been passionately impressed with. He told him he didn't see him as a pop idol, but an 'ordinary bloke idol'. However, Cowell did notice that Rhodes had a good personality and was always good value with Ant and Dec during their post-performance chats. Rhodes's career since the show has followed an appropriate path. He teamed up with fellow finalist Nixon and, playing on their 'ordinary blokes' persona, they became the television presenting duo known as Sam and Mark, not unlike *Pop Idol* presenters Ant and Dec.

As for Cowell, he planned at this stage to step away from television work for a while. He was still enjoying success aplenty with his non-television-related pop acts – Westlife, for instance, had just enjoyed their third number one album, a greatest hits collection. He predicted there would 'probably' be another series of *Pop Idol*, but he wasn't at all sure he wanted to take part if there was. He was, he wrote, feeling 'judged out'. He also said that he suspected the public had had enough of him for the time being. Who would have predicted then that within a matter of months he would be back judging auditions on a new UK talent show that was set to become even bigger and better than *Pop Idol*? Only this time, he would be much more than just a judge.

First, however, the ever ambitious Cowell wanted to crack America...

# CHAPTER FIVE

# AN AMERICAN DREAM

*Question:* What do Simon Cowell and America have in common?
*Answer:*   Simon Cowell loves Simon Cowell... and so does America.

Such is Cowell's fame Stateside nowadays that it's worth recounting his journey to the top from the start, as for a while it seemed quite unlikely that he would make it big over there. With *Pop Idol* proving such a success in the UK, Cowell and his fellow executives quickly decided to pitch the formula to American television networks. It seemed a no-brainer that they would sell it easily, since the show epitomized the 'American dream' with its democratic approach to fame. Here, surely, was a television format that was tailor-made for American audiences. Except that when Cowell flew over to America with Simon Fuller and television producer Simon Jones in the autumn of 2001, midway through the filming of the first series of *Pop Idol*, they initially met with a wall of indifference. Their first meeting was with an unnamed medium-sized television network. Cowell confidently led the pitch to three executives. At the conclusion of his speech, there was a lengthy uneasy silence in the room and the answer was a firm 'no'. Cowell was far from bowed by this rejection, though, and as they left the building, he giggled and told his colleague that this was not the right place for the show anyway. Surely, he thought, the meeting they had set up with a larger television network the following day would be more successful.

Cowell had his doubts when, the following day, they were made to wait for an hour in reception at the network offices. Eventually they were led to a tiny room where Cowell delivered his pitch. He was interrupted midway when the executive held up his hand, indicating that he wanted Cowell to stop. It was exactly the same body language Cowell used to interrupt *Pop Idol* auditions, and he wasn't overjoyed to be on the receiving end. He asked whether he could continue and was told that no, he could not continue, and no, the network were not interested in the idea. Cowell asked why not. 'Because it's a music show,' sighed the executive. Cowell was astounded and had one more go at convincing the executive, who then repeated in the clearest terms that the network were not interested in the *Idol* concept. This time, as they left, Cowell was not in the mood to laugh off the rejection.

He was shocked at American's indifference to the concept and his weariness was compounded by the fact that he'd forgotten to arrange a car to collect him and Jones from the meeting. Suddenly, America seemed a less inviting place. The land of opportunitiy was not sensing one in the *Idol* concept. However, when he and Jones reported back to Fuller, the latter encouraged them to not be disheartened. He still believed strongly that they would sell *Idol* to an American network, though Cowell took some convincing. As he flew home from Los Angeles he might have reflected that when he travelled there with Ellis Rich in the early days of E&S Records, he had left convinced that much would come from his trip, and nothing did. Could it be that despite his despondency, this time the process would be reversed? What seemed like a negative trip might ultimately lead to enormous success?

During 2001, Cowell and Fuller also pitched the show to the Fox television network. According to *The New York Times* television critic Bill Carter, the Fox executives present at the meeting were Sandy Grushow, head of entertainment at Fox, and his chief lieutenant, Gail Berman. Their response was tepid, but the meeting wasn't to be the end of the matter. Fox owner Rupert Murdoch was contacted by his daughter, Elisabeth, who was then heading up BSkyB. She was a fan of *Pop Idol* and told her powerful father that it would be a great format for an American audience. Mr Murdoch then phoned News Corporation's President, Peter Chernin, and asked him what the latest news was on the *Idol* pitch. 'We're still looking at it,' said Chernin. Murdoch's order was simple and direct, 'Don't look at it! Buy it!' The Simons had a deal – *Idol* had a home in America on Fox, one of the biggest networks in the States, and the show would be called *American Idol*.

The next challenge for Cowell was to decide whether or not he wanted to be a judge on *American Idol*. Fox recognized the key role he played on *Pop Idol* and they were keen for him to reprise it on the American show. The thought of a well-spoken Englishman delivering damning verdicts in politically correct America was tantalizing and they were convinced he would be a hit. Cowell? He wasn't so sure. When they first asked him to be a judge he quickly accepted, but then changed his mind and told them he didn't want to judge this time. He was exhausted after *Pop Idol* and wasn't overly keen on the idea of going through the entire process yet again, and in a country much larger than the UK. Judging *American Idol* was going to be an enormous undertaking, he could tell, and he wasn't sure he wanted to do it. His turnaround from an initial 'yes' to subsequent 'no' didn't go down well at Fox. Eventually, though, a friend convinced Cowell that he should be a judge and Fox put their annoyance to one side and accepted him back on board. He had very come close to missing the boat, just as he had when *Popstars* was launched in the UK in 2000. This time, though, he was on board and ready to sail.

Everything looked set for Cowell to take America by storm. After all, there was a recent precedent of a rude Brit going down a treat on US television. Anne Robinson's impolite treatment of contestants on *The Weakest Link* was a key reason for the show's success. Her icy demeanour and put-downs had become legendary, as had her catchphrase, 'You are the weakest link – goodbye.' She was voted the rudest woman on television by readers of *Radio Times* magazine, just one of many such gongs she was awarded. In June 2001, Robinson recorded a pilot episode of the show for the American network NBC and executives were mesmerized by her performance. They snapped her up to front the American version of the show. Robinson was delighted and said, 'My role makes *Dynasty*'s Joan Collins, the last British bitch to appear on American TV, look like Mother Teresa.' Although early reviews of the show Stateside were unfavourable, Robinson soon became a hit in America, where audiences found her demeanour made for irresistible viewing.

Although Cowell has since said he dislikes Robinson and *The Weakest Link*, he was about to make exactly the same sort of impact when he started filming *American Idol*. First, though, he had to meet his fellow judges, with whom he would enjoy widely varying fortunes during their early encounters. The first co-judge he met was Randy Jackson. A man steeped in the music industry, Jackson was born in Louisiana in 1956. He's a loveable mountain of a man, who has been a singer, musician, manager, producer and A&R man. He and Cowell hit it off instantly, the latter saying that within seconds of meeting Jackson he knew they were going to get on famously. Jackson's positive, happy personality does indeed shine through, and it was quickly clear that he and Cowell would get on well both on and off screen. He has since described his rapport with Jackson as akin to the one he has enjoyed for so long with Pete Waterman.

It wasn't until the following day – the first day of filming – that Cowell met his other co-judge, Paula Abdul. Born in 1962, Abdul has made a name for herself as a pop star, record producer, dancer and actress, enjoying a couple of UK Top Five albums and hits such as 'Straight Up' in 1988 and 'Opposites Attract' in 1989. When she and Cowell first met everything went smoothly enough, though Cowell found her a little reserved. Before filming could commence, though, the issue of the fourth judge had to be resolved. Fox producers had been keen to follow the *Pop Idol* format wholesale, which meant a panel of four judges. However, as Cowell recounts, he considered all the people they suggested for the role of fourth judge totally inappropriate. He is kind enough to not mention them by name, but describes one of the candidates as 'Mr Grey'. A magazine journalist from Manhattan,

'Mr Grey' liked to talk about musical credibility and other muso stuff. Cowell described Grey to Lythgoe as possibly the most boring man he had ever met. A second candidate was found and introduced to Cowell. He was a long-haired man in his fifties who Cowell thought looked like an ageing rock roadie and he made Cowell feel incredibly uncomfortable, so he too was dismissed. In the end it was decided that they would go ahead with just three judges.

It wasn't just with the judging panel that Fox were keen to replicate the *Pop Idol* formula; they also decided on a pair of presenters, shadowing Ant and Dec's co-presenting duties in the UK version. However, as Cowell soon concluded, Ant and Dec's rapport is not easy to replicate. The two presenters in America were to be a comedian called Brian Dunkleman and a radio DJ named Ryan Seacrest. Cowell wasn't impressed with the pairing. He thought Seacrest was an enthusiastic asset to the show, with a quick sense of humour and a strangely British persona. He was not, however, enamoured with Dunkleman at all. 'While it's true that many comedians aren't funny when they're off stage,' he wrote in his autobiography, 'Brian went one better – I didn't think he was funny onstage either.' Cowell also got the impression that, in contrast to the effervescent Seacrest, Dunkleman wasn't particularly excited about being part of the show.

For the first series, Dunkleman and Seacrest would co-host the show, and joining Cowell on the judges' panel would be Abdul and Jackson. The scene was set, now all they needed were the contestants. Fortunately they flocked to the auditions. In a land where fame and ambition rule, *American Idol* auditions proved a huge draw. The first auditions were held in Los Angeles, and it quickly became clear that there was going to be a problem between Cowell and Abdul. The first contestant came in and sang – badly in Cowell's opinion – but before he could speak, the other two judges gave their verdicts. Jackson told the singer, 'Yeah, that was a little bit pitchy... but I kinda liked it.' Then Abdul said, 'I loved your audition and I admire your spirit. I don't know if it's quite the voice we're looking for, but I really like you.' These were not the sort of bland responses that Cowell, who described the show as 'a modern-day version of the lions and the Christians', was about to emulate.

He took a deep breath and prepared to deliver his first verdict on American television. 'I think that we have to tell the truth here, which is that this singer is just awful,' he said. 'Not only do you look terrible, but you sound terrible. You're never going to be a pop star in a million years.' America – welcome to the words of Simon Cowell. The shock was palpable as the contestant left the room, then Abdul turned to Cowell with a look of horror and anger on her face. She was appalled by his words and took him to task, asking him who he thought he was, speaking to a contestant so directly. 'This is America,' she reminded him. The pair exchanged words and Abdul grew increasingly more exasperated at Cowell's insistence that he had every right to be honest with contestants and that he planned to continue to do so. Sure enough, the next two contestants were also terrible singers and received similarly direct feedback from Cowell. Abdul's shock and upset at Cowell's honesty was beginning to trouble the programme-makers. During the mid-morning break, Cowell expressed a fear that she was going to walk out on the show. Lythgoe suggested they try to keep her onboard until lunch and then review the situation, at which point they found her sitting behind the scenes in tears. She told Cowell she was devastated by how the morning had gone and that she couldn't stay on the show.

It had been anything but plain sailing for Cowell and *American Idol* thus far. No one could have predicted during that lunchtime what a success the show would go on to become, but in the short term, things weren't going to get much better.

Cowell was very disappointed by the quality of the contestants in the first three cities they visited: Los Angeles, Seattle and Chicago. Then they flew into New York, where further sparks flew between him and Abdul. A contestant called Milk sang 'Sweet Caroline' by Neil Diamond in a jokey cabaret style. Cowell was totally unimpressed by the performance and walked out, followed by Jackson, leaving Abdul alone to decide whether Milk should go through. Fearful that she might put him through, Cowell and Jackson intervened to stop it happening. Abdul was deeply hurt, feeling they were undermining her authority. There were tears and tantrums off camera, and Lythgoe gently sweet-talked her into a calmer state. All the same, she was given the afternoon off to recover. Midway through the afternoon, though, she returned to the set, but the iciness between her and Cowell showed no sign of abating. 'It's all gone a bit mad as far as I'm concerned,' he said. 'I've got a return flight booked; I'm ready to leave if the wrong thing happens.' He felt he was the only sincere judge on the panel because he was honest to the contestants' faces.

The next stop for the auditions was Atlanta. Cowell was getting to know America very well as the *American Idol* auditions took him all round the country. He was also getting to know how difficult Abdul could be when she was upset. Before they flew to Atlanta he noticed that she was very cold towards him and she refused to speak to him during the flight. Sure enough, on the first day of the Atlanta auditions the icy silence erupted into an argument. Abdul told a singer – who Cowell felt had no talent – that if he took singing lessons he could go far. Cowell told her, 'I think you're patronizing this guy,' adding 'he's wasting his life.' Abdul angrily denied she was being patronizing and walked out. At this point, the chances of Cowell and Abdul burying their differences seemed decidedly slender. A meeting was called between the judges and producers that evening in the hope of resolving the conflict. Cowell explained that he wasn't asking Abdul to change her approach, but that she had to accept his style, too. The meeting ended with the conflict essentially resolved. All three judges now knew where they stood and respected – mostly – each other's style of delivering feedback.

Which was just as well, because Cowell was not about to soften his verdicts. He told one singer, 'You have wasted everyone's time, and it's not just a "no", it's a never.' Another was told, 'That was possibly the worst audition I have ever heard. Not only can you not sing; you have a very strange sound.' Speaking of strange sounds, one could only pity the contestant who Cowell informed, 'That sounded like Stevie Wonder with a really bad cold.' He told one singer she sounded like a ship sinking and, sticking with the nautical theme, dispatched yet another by saying, 'If your lifeguard duties were as good as your singing, a lot of people would be drowning.' Appearances, too, were deemed fair game by Cowell. 'You dress better than you sing,' he told one contestant, while another was informed 'you got dressed in the dark.' He was on fine form, informing a disappointed auditionee, 'You sing like Mickey Mouse on helium.' He and Abdul might have buried the hatchet but she was still stunned by much of Cowell's feedback.

'When you entered this competition, did you really believe that you could become what you're standing on, the *American Idol*?' Cowell asked a singer, pointing at the logo on the floor. The contestant said yes, he did believe it. 'Well then, you're deaf,' continued Cowell. 'Thank you, goodbye,' he concluded. Abdul was stunned by his confident, straight-talking style. She had never heard anything quite like it before. Neither had America, where Cowell quickly became a major talking point. 'Simon Cowell is an asshole,' wrote Rob Walker on the influential online magazine *Slate*. 'That's what he's famous for: the needlessly brutal insults of the more hapless contestants on the fame-seeking spectacle *American Idol*. Cowell represents the asshole as truth-teller.'

Fortunately, after the disappointing early stages, some good contestants started auditioning. One such singer was Justin Guarini, who sang 'Who's Loving You'. Abdul described it as a 'wonderful, joyful audition'. However, it was Cowell who really complimented Guarini. 'This is the point at which I'm going to admit that the American talent is probably better than the English talent.' He smiled and then added, 'Justin, you know, occasionally you're very privileged when you do a competition like this to hear somebody undiscovered who has a voice like yours. This is one of those moments – amazing.' However, he was even more impressed by Tamyra Gray in Atlanta. 'The way you look, the way you sing – I thought it was one of the best we've seen today,' he told her. 'Amazing,' he continued, 'this girl may have just started the Z factor because she goes beyond X – it was superb.' He has since said that Gray's was one of the best auditions he has heard on any show. On the same day, RJ Helton auditioned, singing 'Never Can Say Goodbye'. After Abdul had roundly praised Helton, Cowell said, 'I have to agree – which I don't do very often. You look good, you sound good… I think this competition's for you.' Another singer called EJay Day also impressed.

In Dallas, Texas, a twenty-year-old woman called Kelly Clarkson auditioned. Before she went into the audition room, the nine previous contestants had left in tears after being dismissed by the judges. She admits she was expecting Cowell to 'yell' at her. She sang well and then made the judges laugh by agreeing to swap places with Jackson so the judge could audition for the singer. 'You could be a star,' joked Clarkson. Cowell grinned as he took the chance to have a dig at Jackson, saying, 'Not in a billion, trillion years should he go through.' Returning to the question of Clarkson's audition, all three judges put her through to the next stage, Cowell saying his 'yes' vote was dependent on her telling Seacrest that he needed to re-do his highlights. It was a challenge she accepted, and she admitted later she was relieved that 'the British guy didn't make me cry'. She embraced Cowell before she left and delivered the requested putdown to Seacrest. Cowell, listening from the audition room, roared with laughter. It had been a memorable audition, but perhaps more so for Clarkson's personality than her voice. At this stage, Cowell expected Gray and Guarini to be the top two musical talents to emerge from the series.

However, as the show progressed to the next round in Hollywood, Clarkson began to emerge as a major contender. She went through to the final ten, and at this stage the front-runners appeared to be Gray, Guarini and Clarkson. The latter received more praise from Cowell, who pulled off the old feedback twist trick, telling Clarkson, 'America is not known for nice singers, it is known for great singers [pause] and you are one of them. Congratulations.' He told one singer, 'OK, I admit it, I've got a crush' and he told Gray she had pulled off 'one of the best performances on TV I have ever seen'. When he criticized Guarini, the singer brushed off the critique, looking from Cowell to the audience and saying, 'I really respect your opinion, but what do you guys think?'

Cowell was dreaming of a final between Clarkson and Gray. However, in one of the shocks of the series, Gray was voted out three weeks from the final. The audience and judges were stunned, and Abdul told Gray, 'I feel like I've seen Muhammad Ali knocked down for the first time.' Cowell was horrified by the loss of Gray and felt a similar emotion when he learned that for the final (which would be contested by Clarkson and Guarini) he and his fellow judges would not be allowed to speak but would be sitting up in the gods of Hollywood's huge Kodak Theatre. Opened in 2001, the Kodak is a grand venue that has played host to numerous Oscar ceremonies. Cowell was disappointed that he, Abdul and Jackson wouldn't be playing a part in the drama of the final in September 2002. During *Pop Idol*, he had managed to overturn a similar decision, but for the first series of *American Idol* he had to grin and bear it. He did, however, sign up to judge the second series of *American Idol* that very evening.

The final was split over two nights, as pure Hollywood glamour turned it into an even bigger event than the *Pop Idol* final had been. Cowell was hoping for a Clarkson victory and he got it. However, he was disappointed that when her victory was announced, her opponent Guarini, rather than looking crestfallen, jumped and cheered for her. Cowell, with his ultra-competitive nature, has never been able to understand contestants who affect joy on behalf of their opponents. Here, he came up against a side of America he found harder to embrace: political correctness. However, he had already gone a long way to countering that aspect of the American psyche – and he'd become a major star in doing so. Cowell was, it is no exaggeration to say, becoming a superstar in the United States of America.

As *American Idol* rolled out, Cowell's fame – or infamy – in America rose and rose. He became a major talking point across the nation, as some of America's most prestigious publications reflected. The *Wall Street Journal* said, 'Simon Cowell's judgements may be stern, but they are sharp and his stardom attests to the fact that, deep down, Americans still hunger for the truth. Funny that it takes a Brit to remind us.' *The New York Times*, too, felt that Cowell was performing a public service. 'In an age when parents aren't able to confront their children's shortcomings, it seems like Cowell is the only one who will,' said the newspaper. *USA Today* applauded him. 'Cowell is the greatest British export since The Beatles,' it cheered. As for *Time* magazine, it said, 'Simon Cowell is the Barry Goldwater [outspoken American politician] of reality TV: in your heart, you know he's right.' It added, 'Simon Cowell has changed the way in which we think about television in the US.'

He had indeed. Many Americans were relieved that Cowell had arrived in their country and waged a one-man campaign against the pandering political correctness that predominated. The feeling was summed up by Hannah Jones, in the *Western Mail*: 'He's the antithesis of the "You're beautiful and talented just the way you are, but you might not want to give up the day job" political correctness this country once fawned over. The song "Cruel To Be Kind" could have been written for him because he's the man who, literally, tells it like it is.' Naturally, as a man who did just that, Cowell had to endure some criticisms coming back at him. The high trousers might have gone, but he still faced digs about his appearance. On the American show *HDTV News*, commentator Phillip Swann said, 'Fox Television needs to lighten up on that white concealer under his eyes. It's supposed to reduce on-camera puffiness, but it sometimes makes Cowell look like a racoon.' Writing in the *Dallas Morning News*, Ed Bark said of Cowell, 'He wears muscle shirts to accessorize his overall vanity.'

He had extra fuel for his vanity when Clarkson's debut single went to number one in the Billboard chart in its first week on sale. Ultimately it sold over one million copies. Cowell had predicted just such sales for the winners' single before the series began and hadn't been believed by the record company, RCA, which was to put out the single. The fact that the song did so well was vindication of *American Idol* and of Cowell himself. The single was called 'A Moment Like This' and Clarkson was not the only artist Cowell would have a hit with via that song. For the moment, though, he could bask in the glory of Clarkson's hit and his own part in *American Idol*'s success. The process had endured a very rocky start, but the show had proved to be a big hit.

Just six weeks after Clarkson was crowned champion of series one, Cowell and the crew began filming series two. The format was much the same, though to Cowell's relief Dunkleman didn't return, leaving Seacrest as the sole presenter. On the opening show of the series, Cowell dispelled any hopes that he wouldn't be as tough-talking this time around. 'I promise one thing,' he said, 'I will be a lot tougher on the contestants than I was last year. Honestly, they got off lightly. Truthfully, they got off lightly. I remember sitting there towards the end and thinking, I am so biting my tongue at the moment. Because if I say what I want to say, I might be thrown out of America.' He was given plenty of ammunition by the contestants. As with the second series of *Pop Idol*, many arrived for the auditions prepared to make a mockery of the process. One came dressed as Tarzan, another as the Lion King. Others arrived dressed as everything from vegetables and lizards to Klingons from the *Star Trek* series.

Most pranksters were given short shrift by Cowell, who saw them coming a mile off. However, one practical joke that was aimed specifically at Cowell took a little longer for him to spot. A moody twenty-two-year-old singer arrived and said that he was so nervous he wanted to bring his brother in to audition with him. With the duo complete, they performed an atrocious, comical rap version of 'Opposites Attract'. At first Cowell sat back in his seat with his arms folded and rolled his eyes. Then the pair started break-dancing, and at this point, a look of recognition crossed Cowell's face. Then he smiled, held up his hands and said, 'OK guys, OK!' He had recognized who the two young men were – Ant and Dec in disguise. He sat back in his chair laughing and said, 'Oh my God!' As everyone on the set howled with laughter, Cowell said, 'I don't fucking believe it! Oh brilliant!' He embraced the pair and applauded them for pulling off the stunt so well.

*

Although Cowell and Abdul were getting on much better in series two, there was still a tension between them. In the latter stages of series one, she had hired a comedy scriptwriter to give her ripostes to Cowell's put-downs. Naturally, this just prompted Cowell to create a new set of put-downs. 'Paula,' he said, 'it sounds like you have a comedy writer. Please sue him.' In series two, she came up with a new method of coping with Cowell, with similarly disastrous results. During the New York auditions he noted that she had a pile of cushions on her chair to make her seem taller. Concluding she had done this as a kind of one-upmanship, he waited till she left the room and ordered a pile of cushions for himself and Jackson to place on their chairs. He also took to occasionally lowering her seat while she was out of the room.

As well as these stealth tactics, Cowell jousted verbally with Abdul. One day he complained to an auditionee, 'I'm just so bored today.' Abdul sighed and said, 'I could stand naked in front of you... and you'd still be bored.' Without missing a beat, Cowell replied, 'I would agree with you, if you stood naked in front of me I wouldn't be excited.' He was similarly swift in responding to jibes from angry contestants. 'You know what?' protested one singer who had been rejected by Cowell, 'at least I live in a country where people brush their teeth twice a day!' Cowell shrugged and said, 'Gosh, that told me.' Another contestant shouted at Cowell, 'You're horrible!' To which Cowell replied, 'So are you.' Completely disarmed, the contestant calmly said, 'Fine.'

Drama of an entirely different nature unfolded when Lythgoe, the executive producer of the show and a friend of Cowell, suffered a heart attack in Los Angeles as preparations began for the second series. He had holidayed in Barbados over

Christmas (as had Cowell) and had complained of chest pains. Once in Los Angeles he was taken to hospital. Cowell had the news broken to him by Ken Warwick, the show's executive producer. For several worried days he kept in close contact with Lythgoe's family. This was the man who had kickstarted Cowell's reality-TV career when he invited him to be a judge on *Popstars* back in 2000. Though Cowell had turned the offer down, indirectly it had led to everything that had happened to him since. After some days, Lythgoe recovered and was released from hospital. 'And in true Nigel Lythgoe style,' wrote Cowell in his autobiography, 'he was back at work within three weeks. No one could stop him.'

Someone who was stopped in their tracks, though, was contestant Frenchie Davis. She had first auditioned in New York, having queued in a line that snaked across six Manhattan blocks. A large black woman with bright blonde hair, she sang 'I Am Telling You' with powerful soul. All three judges responded to her audition with a round of applause. 'See you in Hollywood,' said Cowell, clearly impressed. Here, he believed, was the winner of series two. However, as the series approached its live shows it was discovered that Davis had once posed topless for an adult website. Lythgoe phoned Cowell to break the news about the photographs. After weeks of mulling over their options, Fox decided that due to the family nature of the show, Davis would have to be removed from the competition. Cowell felt sympathy for her.

Another contestant who was voted out was Corey Clark, when it was revealed he was facing criminal charges of assault. This revelation came during the live shows, which meant that one week no contestants were eliminated.

Thankfully, there was a decent flow of talented, clean-cut contestants, too. These included Ruben Studdard, a mountainous man with a sweet soul voice and loveable personality, and the geeky Clay Aiken, another young man with a huge aura. Joshua Gracin also stood out due to his background in the Marines. Eventually, after a wildcard round, the field was whittled down to a top twelve. Pleased as he was with some of the talent in the running, Cowell was less than delighted when he learned that Fox were appointing a 'celebrity judge' to join the panel for each of the live shows. When the production team told him this was the plan, he was openly dismissive: 'If you think it's such a good idea,' he told them, 'then why don't you bring a celebrity executive producer in next week?' They didn't appreciate the way he made the point. He then went to the press and was open about his feelings with them.

The celebrity judges included singer Gladys Knight, Olivia Newton-John, Neil Sedaka, Bee Gees singer Robin Gibb and Earth, Wind & Fire bassist Verdine White. Cowell still wasn't sold on the idea, but when the legendary Lionel Richie joined the panel it worked far better. Cowell enjoyed Richie's sharpness and humour. When one of the contestants sang a Richie song, Richie told him he'd sang it nearly as well as his original version. Cowell followed this up saying, 'Well, with respect, Lionel, I never particularly liked your original.' Richie, as sharp as ever, realized Cowell was joking but went along with it, feigning outrage at Cowell's comment. The pair carried on the joke for some weeks, pretending to be at odds with each other.

As the final neared, Cowell was secretly hoping it would be contested by Studdard and Aiken. To help them along, when he felt either singer was becoming complacent, he gave them a pep talk. In Studdard's case, this feedback shocked the audience. However, backstage Studdard approached Cowell and thanked him for his comments, which he felt were justified and helpful. Cowell, who had noted the charismatic effect Studdard had on other contestants, was impressed and began to see in him a winner. Aiken, too, he felt, was a major contender, and as each week went by and both of them survived elimination, Cowell's dream final seemed more likely. There was one nervous moment when Studdard was in the dreaded bottom two, but he survived to fight another day and made it to the final. So, too, did Aiken, despite a scare when he sang 'Grease'. The performance is best summed up by Cowell himself, who told the singer, 'If I had been watching this on TV, I would actually have run out of the room. This was a perfect example of how a performer can go from amazing to awful. The red leather outfit, the ghastly winks, the horrible hip dance: to say it was dreadful is an understatement.'

Aiken survived the scare and lined up to compete alongside Studdard in the final, which was once again to be held over two nights at the Kodak Theatre in Hollywood. This time round the excitement and hype surrounding the final was even bigger than in series one. Cowell spoke to both contestants backstage, but he had the feeling that, due to nerves, his advice had fallen on deaf ears. Each singer performed three songs. The highlight for Studdard came when he sang 'Flying Without Wings', complete with a gospel choir backing him. As Cowell watched the particular performance he felt enormous personal pride. He had enjoyed a number one hit with the song with Westlife in 1999, and when Gareth Gates had sung the song on *Pop Idol* he had put himself, the show and Cowell on the map. Now here he sat in Hollywood as another singer belted out the song's inspirational lyrics on *American Idol*.

Aiken then performed the final song of the evening, 'Bridge Over Troubled Water'. He nailed the song and Cowell remembers the hairs standing up on the back of his neck as he watched. As the song ended, he felt sure that Aiken was going to win. When he saw both singers backstage afterwards, their body language suggested that they too believed Aiken would be the winner. However, when he reviewed the performances on tape later, he concluded that Studdard would win. The following evening, after a hectic day at the Cowell household, it was time for the result show, which was watched by fifty million Americans. Before the result was announced, the judges – who were given a role after further protests from Cowell over their exclusion in the final of series one – were invited to offer a final word to the contestants. After Jackson and Abdul offered their thoughts, it was time for Cowell to speak. He laughed and said, 'I still don't understand a single word you say, Paula. You talk rubbish! All I would say is, we said in this competition earlier on, it's image versus talent. Talent won, America got it right. Seriously, guys, congratulations.' Studdard was then voted the winner. Cowell stood up and clapped, smiling with a look of sheer joy on his face. Aiken, he noticed, was less joyful, and Cowell noted that in contrast to the previous series' runner-up, he couldn't hide his disappointment. It was all far more in keeping with Cowell's ultra-competitive view of the world.

It was a view that was being increasingly satisfied by Cowell's growing success. His mutual love affair with America was

Cowell with his operatic quartet Il Divo, who signed to his label in 2003 and have since released five top-selling albums.

Besides women, Cowell is passionate about cars. Here he is leaning against his Bentley, outside his Beverly Hills home in 2004.

Sharing a giggle with the *X Factor* team at the British Comedy Awards in 2005 (from l-r, presenter Kate Thornton, Cowell, judges Sharon Osbourne and Louis Walsh).

In his acceptance speech for a TV award in 2004, Cowell thanked two people: his mum, and publicist Max Clifford. The latter is pictured here with Cowell outside Cipriani in 2006.

As well as receiving awards, Cowell likes to give back. Here he is next to Sir Elton John at the *Billy Elliot* Charity Gala in 2006 – perhaps he has inherited his mother's talent for ballet?

Posing for the PDSA charity calendar in 2007.

World class: winner of the third series of *The X Factor* in 2006, Leona Lewis is now an internationally-renowned recording artist.

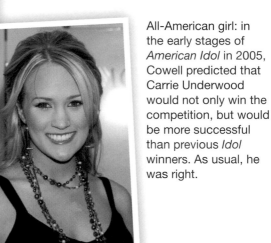

All-American girl: in the early stages of *American Idol* in 2005, Cowell predicted that Carrie Underwood would not only win the competition, but would be more successful than previous *Idol* winners. As usual, he was right.

Will going strong: winner of the original *Pop Idol*, Will Young remains one of the talent show format's biggest success stories.

Cowell's brainchild *America's Got Talent* first aired in 2006 and was won by eleven-year-old singer Bianca Ryan (pictured). Despite being involved in producing the show, Cowell does not appear as a judge.

Prince Charming: meeting the Queen at the Royal Variety Performance in 2007, with fellow *Britain's Got Talent* judge Amanda Holden (right).

From Carphone Warehouse to Downing Street: *BGT* 2007 was won by phone salesman-cum-opera singer Paul Potts, seen here having tea with Cowell and Prime Minister Gordon Brown.

While judging *American Idol* in 2007, Cowell received an unexpected visitor. He was presented with the *This Is Your Life* red book by Sir Trevor McDonald.

The first 'victim' of the re-launched programme, Cowell was joined by his mum Julie and brother Nicholas in the studio.

This is the high life: Cowell can count Kate Moss among his celebrity friends.

The walk of fame: Cowell receives the Special Recognition
Award at the National Television Awards in 2008.

'The woman who shut up Simon Cowell': *BGT* contestant
Susan Boyle silenced the judges in her 2009 audition, and
became an overnight Internet sensation, with 2.5 million
views on YouTube in the first 72 hours.

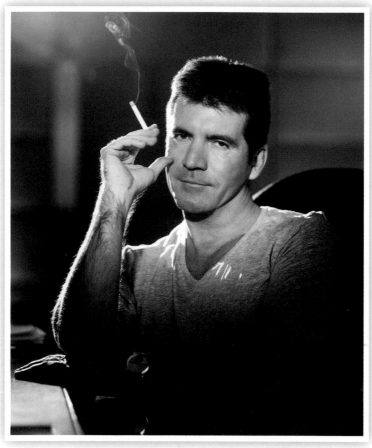

Smoking hot: the businessman, the judge, the celebrity …
Simon Cowell remains one of the most influential players in
the entertainment industry.

deepening. America really got Simon Cowell. As *The Los Angeles Times* put it, 'Simon's ego is so large it is the only man-made object that can be seen from space.' Such was his profile in America that he was invited to play a cameo role on the film *Scary Movie 3*, the third instalment of the horror movie parody franchise, directed by David Zucker. During a rap-off scene in a club between two rival hip-hoppers, Cowell appears and is asked to give his verdict. Arms folded and wearing his trademark black jumper, he says, 'I thought you were both absolutely dreadful – ghastly.' He then stands up and, looking round the crowded venue, says, 'I don't know what I'm doing here. This club is totally pathetic.' The rappers on the stage then pull out guns and shoot at Cowell, who collapses on the floor. It wasn't a prestigious performance, Cowell was merely being himself. Neither was it one that he was keen to repeat. He told ITV2's Kate Thornton that he believed there was a line beyond which it was ungracious for celebrities to push their fame, 'and with *Scary Movie 3* I think I might have crossed that line,' he confessed with a smile. His performance was, though, confirmation of his status in America. As a Brit, to be awarded a role in a top Hollywood movie is clear recognition of one's standing in the United States.

One commentator who urges some perspective when assessing Cowell's popularity in America is British writer Toby Young, who documented his own attempts to make it as a Brit in the States in his bestselling book *How to Lose Friends and Alienate People*, which has since been adapted into a Hollywood film. Young suspects that Cowell is, despite the hype, not the best-known Englishman in America. 'He's probably not better known than the Queen or Winston Churchill,' he shrugs, 'though I could be wrong.' Young adds, 'He must have been pretty chuffed that President Obama gave him a name check on Leno. I'm not sure Obama could have made a gag referencing any other British celebrity that everyone would have instantly got.' Some have said that with his white teeth, Botox and permatan, Cowell has 'gone native' since working in Hollywood. Young says it was always thus. 'I think he has always been what Tom Wolfe described as a "mid-Atlantic man", only without the mid-Atlantic accent.'

Young also contests the view expressed in some quarters that Cowell is the true star of *American Idol*. 'I'm not sure the reason ordinary Americans tune in to the show is to see Cowell's mug on their screens,' he says. 'The prevailing wisdom on these sorts of reality shows – and I'm sure Cowell would agree – is that it's not about the judges, it's about the contestants. They're the people the public tune in to watch. The role of the judges is to enforce the rules of the competition. They're like referees in a football match. And while Cowell is an excellent referee, I don't think people tune in to see him blowing his whistle, "I don't mean to be rude, but..." they tune in to watch the players strutting their stuff.'

An American who has personal reason to admire Cowell is *American Idol* finalist Anthony Fedorov, who came fourth in season four. At the end of that season's finale, he enjoyed an inspirational backstage conversation with Cowell. 'I came into his dressing room to say goodbye and to thank him for the experience,' recalls Fedorov with a smile. 'He sat me down and told me that I had a lot of talent and that I needed to discover who I was as an artist. He said: "Right now you need to crawl under a rock for the next few years and work on your artistry and get better, because you have a lot of potential. Once you understand who you are, you will re-emerge and be very successful." I took that to heart and I believe now I am ready to be a star because I finally know who I am.'

The boyish Fedorov is an all-round fan of Cowell. 'He is much nicer in person than on camera,' he says firmly. 'But I never found him to be mean on camera either. He is just brutally honest. He knows music. He knows what he wants and won't settle for anything less. My experience with him was great. I never got offended by anything he said. I agreed with him most of the time.' Fedorov confirms that Cowell remains a major icon in the United States.

Back in 2003 after the climax of season two, Cowell obviously felt comfortable with his stature in America. So much so that he signed up for a further series of *American Idol*. 'I have a real problem with boredom,' he says in *I Hate to be Rude, But...* 'I also have a massive fear about not being in control of my own destiny. The great thing about this show is that, for the next two or three years, I have a way of controlling my destiny.' Back home in England, he had thought of a way of taking that control over his destiny to even greater levels. Throughout his judgements on *Pop Idol* and *American Idol*, he had told contestants that if they wanted to win the show, they had to have that elusive quality – the X factor. It was a phrase that would take his fame to even greater heights in his home country.

# CHAPTER SIX

# X MARKS THE SPOT

In 2004, having enjoyed the success of *Pop Idol* in the UK and *American Idol* in the US, Cowell decided to form a new company, Syco, an independently run division within his long-time employer BMG (which then became Sony BMG and is now called Sony Music Entertainment). Ever ambitious and competitive, he wasn't willing to rest on his laurels in the face of his *Pop Idol* success. For him, the fame of appearing on the show and the fortune of signing the winner to his record label was not enough. He wanted not so much a bigger slice of the cake, but the rights to the *whole* cake. Through the production company Syco, he hoped to achieve just that. Based in an unexciting office block near the River Thames in west London, Syco has three departments: Syco Music, Syco TV and Syco Film. Cowell opted to keep the team small but effective, claiming in 2006 in *The Telegraph* that 'our little division, Syco Music [employing just fourteen staff], last year accounted for something like 40 per cent of Sony BMG's profit, and they employ four hundred people'. (By 2009 *The Times* was claiming Syco employed twenty people and accounted for 70 per cent of its parent company's profits.) Betraying both his sense of humour and his ego, outside his office stands a life-size cardboard cut-out of the cartoon Cowell from his February 2004 appearance on *The Simpsons*. He played an admissions officer at a nursery school who hurls insults at all the toddlers who apply. 'It's the best thing I've ever been asked to do,' he'd said after recording his voice track for the show.

The first project to emerge from Syco was *The X Factor*, which was to take the reality music television show to a whole new level. Cowell had enormous leverage when he pitched the show to ITV. The second series of *Pop Idol* had failed to grab the imagination of the public to the same extent as series one, and had produced a less enthralling top two contestants. It had become clear to ITV that Cowell was the real star of the format, so they were well disposed to his overtures that *The X Factor* should replace *Pop Idol*.

The new format was simple, retaining some of the old elements of *Pop Idol* but introducing new ideas too. Open auditions were to be held across the country where anyone over the age of sixteen could compete in front of a three-person panel. It wasn't just solo artists who would be allowed to perform, but groups too. If two out of the three judges gave an act a 'yes' vote, that act would make it through to the next round, known as boot-camp. The next round would see each of the three judges awarded a category of contestant to mentor for the remainder of the series: the sixteen- to twenty-four-year-olds, the over-twenty-five-year-olds and the groups. The judges would invite the acts in their category to their homes, and after further eliminations, a top-three in each category would be picked to form a final nine. They would compete on live shows on Saturday nights in front of a studio audience and millions of viewers. At this stage, the public vote would come into play, and each week an act would be eliminated until a winner was crowned. That winner would be given a million-pound recording contract.

Here, in many ways, Cowell had created the ultimate reality music show. There were many new aspects to the concept, including allowing bands and over twenty-five-year-old artists to compete. However, the change that really gave the show a whole new dimension was giving the judges roles as mentors, as this gave the proceedings a distinctly competitive edge in the second half of the series. Indeed, the judges became as much competitors as the acts themselves. Some commentators linked this aspect of the show to a recent reality show, which Cowell had not participated in, called *Popstars: The Rivals*. On that show, two rival judges (Pete Waterman and Louis Walsh) mentored rival categories to form a band each. However, it seems more likely that the idea of this mentoring angle came to Cowell during the second series of *Pop Idol*, when he effectively mentored Michelle McManus.

The key component to getting *The X Factor* right – more so than on previous reality shows, due to the mentoring dimension of the show – was the judging panel. Cowell opted for a three-person panel in which he would be joined by his old pal and colleague Louis Walsh and the colourful Sharon Osbourne.

Daughter of controversial music mogul Don Arden, and wife of rock legend Ozzy Osbourne, Sharon Osbourne was a natural choice to become a judge, given her customary candour – she has confessed in her autobiography to numerous scraps with her husband, including one in which she claims he tried to kill her, as well as speaking openly about how she has battled cancer, sent excrement through the post to enemies and spent considerable sums on plastic surgery. Both judges had form in reality television: Walsh had been a judge on *Popstars: The Rivals*, from which he produced the mega-successful Girls Aloud, and Osbourne was well-known for her wild, matriarchal performances on MTV show *The Osbournes*. Cowell summed up the difference between his two co-judges. 'If Sharon were a dog, she would be one of those over-bred Pomeranians – fluffy and feisty – whereas Louis is a kind of mutt dog with big, appealing eyes that knows how to get things,' he said. As for himself, Cowell said, 'I'm more of a cat.'

When *The X Factor* auditions opened, Cowell was like the cat that got the cream. Over 50,000 hopefuls turned up to auditions held in Dublin, Newcastle, London, Leeds, Birmingham and Glasgow during the summer of 2004. There, Cowell was the star of the panel, just as he had been during the *Idol* shows. Again, a high proportion of acts that were awful – by accident or design – showed up, making the early audition phase entertaining viewing. 'I'd say ninety per cent of the people who turned up were awful,' said Cowell looking back over the show. 'We had everything from an eighty-one-year-old granny to a sixty-five-year-old woman trying to pass herself off as a twenty-year-old.' That was only the beginning of the madness. A man turned up dressed as Spiderman and a sixty-seven-year-old retired miner named Mario sang the most bizarre opera ever. Amid all the craziness, Cowell was on majestic verbal form, his witty put-downs more hilarious than ever. He told the girl band Caution, 'You look like ice skaters who've been locked up for fifteen years.' When a singer called Paul Holt sang 'End Of My World', Cowell concluded, 'It's the end of your singing career, that's for sure.' And when Josh McGuire sang, Cowell's advice to him was to become 'more of a drag queen'.

He took a similar approach with a camp guy from Essex called Darren, who told the panel, 'I was born in 1890, I died in 1912 and was born again a considerable amount of years later, and here I am now. I suppose you could vaguely call it reincarnation.' Cowell was unimpressed and simply told the male hopeful, 'You look like Princess Diana.' Harsh words, but that was arguably kind compared to the verdict he gave one woman, 'You don't need a judge,' he told her, 'you need an exorcist. I mean seriously, that was weird!' And he told a dancing performer that the performance was akin to 'an audition for "One Flew Over The Cuckoo's Nest".'

With Cowell now nearing national institution status, the contestants were prepared for his acid tongue and often responded in good humour. Often, but not always. Thirtysomething girl band, Sweet Harmony, were furious when the judging panel compared them to 'old slappers'. Cowell told them, 'Individually you sound horrendous, together you sound even worse. I don't think anyone would pay to hear you sing.' The singers stormed out of the audition room and band member Jenny raged, 'I don't look like a slapper. I've been singing professionally for years. That's disgusting what they said to us.' However, their fury was nowhere near as memorable as that of rapper Benjamin, whose response to Cowell's feedback quickly went down in reality-television folklore.

Cowell told the wannabe hip-hopper, 'You have as much credibility as a rapper as George Formby does.' The fuming contestant screamed, 'You wouldn't know talent if it hit you in the face. You're a disgrace.' However, this was only the beginning of the drama, as he then launched into a clearly prepared rap, aimed angrily at Cowell: 'What's your name Simon Cowell, with trousers at your waist. You wouldn't know talent if it hit you in da face. You're a disgrace. You don't know [bleep] about talent apart from bubble gum pop and that's it. Do you think I care about topping the charts – stick that commercial [bleep] up your [bleep].'

Osbourne, who's always up for some verbal pyrotechnics, followed Benjamin out of the room and asked, 'Do you wish you were black?' He replied, 'Do you wish your kids weren't in rehab?' and stormed off. Osbourne was fuming about this personal attack on her family and stormed after him, 'I hate redheads anyway. If he starts again on my kids I'll beat the [bleep] out of him. If he carried on I would have given him a kick up the [bleep], the little [bleep].' She was quickly justifying Cowell's hiring of her as a judge. He wanted the hell-raiser side of her to come to the fore and it was.

A hell of a different kind was threatened when Cowell was issued with a lawsuit from Simon Fuller, the man he had worked with on *Pop Idol*, which led to fears that the entire *X Factor* bandwagon might collapse. After watching the opening show of the series, Fuller said he noted twenty-five similarities between *The X Factor* and *Pop Idol*, including everything from the stage set-up, music, logos and lighting to the way the judges were seated and contestants lined up for the auditions. Fuller's company, 19 Entertainment, which created *Pop Idol* and *American Idol*, launched legal action against producer FremantleMedia, Cowell and his firms Simco and Syco. '19 TV will be pressing for a speedy trial to resolve the matters as swiftly as is possible,' a spokesman from 19 said.

FremantleMedia – whose subsidiary Talkback Thames produces *X Factor* – said in a statement, 'We deny the allegations made in the writ and in the press. We will defend any action vigorously and we hope to resolve the matter amicably.' It added, '*The X Factor* is a different format to *Pop Idol*.' Cowell branded it 'utterly ridiculous'. His spokesman Max Clifford told the BBC, 'Does this mean that Granada could sue the BBC for creating *EastEnders* because it made *Coronation Street* first? Look at *New Faces* and *Opportunity Knocks*, there have always been television talent programmes.' Cowell has since quipped that in his line of work, when you have a hit, you have a writ.

In November 2005, during the filming of the second series of *The X Factor*, Cowell and Fuller settled out of court. 'We're delighted with the outcome. People think we hate each other but we don't. We're good friends,' Cowell said, and added, 'Even throughout the last lawsuit, which probably lasted eighteen months, we must have had dinner on five or six occasions. I knew why he had issued us with the lawsuit and I think he knew why I had launched *X Factor*. There was a kind of understanding that only he and I [had] really and, because we understand both positions, it didn't feel particularly personal. I never thought it was going to go to court, so I treated the whole thing as kind of like paperwork.' It's a separation of the professional and personal spheres that's a key factor in the lives of those who soar.

However, there can be little argument that Cowell was at best opportunistic, at worst downright cheeky when he sold *The X Factor* to ITV. Having made his name on Fuller's show *Pop Idol*, he took the best parts of that format and pulled the rug from under Fuller's feet with *The X Factor*. No wonder Fuller took legal action. However, it is typical of Cowell's rare blend of cheek and charm that he and Fuller have remained both friends and colleagues in spite of this legal battle.

In the first series of *The X Factor*, as fun as the poor contestants and the judges' reactions to them were, Cowell was desperate to find a genuine star. This was the first reality show to be produced by Syco, which meant the stakes could not be higher for him, both for his professional pride and his pocket: the winner of the show would receive a £1 million recording contract with the record division of Syco, and parent company Sony BMG would have first pick of all the live finalists. He didn't have to wait long for the quality to emerge. When operatic boyband G4 first walked into the room, Cowell thought they looked like bankers. 'I'm glad you said bankers,' quipped cheeky Walsh. However, once they began their performance of Queen's 'Bohemian Rhapsody', Cowell and his fellow judges were stunned. 'You are an amazing singer,' he told frontman Jonathan Ansell. 'An amazing singer, amazing singer. Really amazing.' As Ansell choked back the tears, Cowell told them he would happily give them a record deal on the spot. He already had a band not unlike G4 on his label, so it's little wonder he was so enthused by Ansell and the others.

Then came the unforgettable Rowetta Satchell. Then thirty-eight, the Manchester lady had been singing for twenty-five years before she turned up in front of Cowell and his fellow *X Factor* judges. Her CV included backing vocals for a number of bands, including Simply Red and the Happy Mondays, for whom she sang on their iconic 1990 number five hit 'Step On'. Her audition songs were 'Lady Marmalade' and 'Bridge Over Troubled Water' and she quickly caught the attention and hearts of the judges with her eccentric ways. 'Do you stop for air, missus?' asked Osbourne. 'My mum's Jewish, my dad's Nigerian, I've got two King Charles Cavalier spaniels, but I'm not allowed to switch my phone on to show you – please, I'm begging. You can't not put me through, my mum would go mad!' She was put through – with Cowell issuing the casting vote – then she ran down the corridor in celebration. 'I am through!' she screamed. 'Rowetta, you fruit cake,' shouted presenter Kate Thornton as she was running after her. 'Come back!'

Looking back at her *X Factor* experience, Satchell remembers her time with Cowell fondly. 'I learned to believe in myself and my talent more,' she says, smiling. 'Simon was so complimentary towards me, he really boosted my confidence. He genuinely loved my voice and said I was one of the best singers he'd heard in the last twenty years. Coming from Simon, who hears singers all the time, that was amazing.' She adds that the thing she most remembers about him is his humour. 'He is even funnier off camera, and he really does light up a room when he walks in,' she says. She declines to elaborate on specific funny Cowell moments, insisting that private conversations must remain just that. 'I will say that his humour is very dry and a little twisted, which I love about him, and he is very down to earth for someone who must be on his way to being a billionaire. Simon is one of the most charming, charismatic people I've ever met. I also remember the first time he realized I could really sing – "Somewhere Over The Rainbow", at boot-camp – great moment.'

Satchell had long admired Cowell, since watching him on shows like *American Idol*. 'I always thought he'd love my voice and like my personality,' she says. It was only when *The X Factor* – which had no upper age limit – was launched that she had a chance to audition in front of him. 'To be honest, I always thought I'd get on with him, and I still think he's fabulous, on and off screen. I consider myself very lucky to have got to work with him on the first series of his new baby, *The X Factor*.'

Another promising performer was thirty-five-year-old Steve Brookstein. He said it felt 'surreal' to be there, prompting a smile from Cowell. He sang well but the panel seemed to have mixed feelings about him. Cowell and Osbourne identified a rather defeatist air in Brookstein's body language, though Cowell highly praised the singer's voice. He voted to put Brookstein through, but the other two judges said no. The outvoted Cowell said, 'Steve, I've got to tell you, you blew it on the interview. It's a real shame. A real shame.' After Brookstein had left the room, Walsh and Osbourne explained their thinking and Cowell interrupted and said, 'Oh God, can we get him back? Can we get him back?' He threw his pen on the desk in frustration and said, 'I think he's that good.'

When Brookstein returned Cowell said, 'Steve, I'll tell you why we asked you to come back because it's a bit of a split panel.' He went on to tell Brookstein that Walsh thought he 'didn't give a shit'. Brookstein told Walsh, 'You don't know me.' Cowell invited Brookstein to re-audition the next day. After the second audition, Cowell said, 'You're going to need a lot of work, Steve. You're going to need a lot of work.' Nevertheless, the crooner received three 'yes' votes and was through to the next round. Cowell's intervention had saved him from falling at the first hurdle.

One other memorable singer was fifty-year-old Verity Keays. She impressed the judges, though Cowell memorably told her, 'I don't know what to say because I see you in a garden, pruning roses.' However, behind the scenes he reacted emotionally to her audition. 'Even I got touched, and that's rare,' he said, choking back tears. Coming from an emotionally distant man such as Cowell, the reaction spoke volumes.

After the boot-camp stage, each of the three judges were awarded a category. Cowell was given the over twenty-fives category, and put them through their paces at the Landmark Hotel. From there, he chose five acts to go to the 'judges' house' phase. Cowell's sparsely furnished west London house in fashionable Holland Park is a four-storey mansion that was once the residence of an ambassador, with high ceilings and dark wood flooring. He also owns a £15 million mansion in Beverly Hills and properties in Barbados, Malaga and Dubai. However, the beautifully appointed judges' houses featured on the show were in fact rented for the occasion, as a spokeswoman for the show confirmed in 2007 after Louis Walsh came clean on *The Graham Norton Show*.

Whatever the truth, it was in this slightly intimidating setting that the acts had to perform in front of Cowell again, as well as reveal more of their personalities in an informal chat with their mentor. 'How would you feel if you didn't make the finals?' Cowell asked Brookstein, who replied that 'I would be lying if I said I wouldn't be very disappointed'. Cowell glared at Brookstein and told him, 'Now look me in the eye and tell me you think you can win this competition.' Brookstein giggled and said, 'I don't like to boast. I think I can win it.' Cowell, keen to unearth whether this contestant had sufficient self-belief, pointed out that he wasn't looking him in the eye. As a competitive man, Cowell wanted to find plenty of that characteristic in the acts he was mentoring.

Having heard them sing and listened to them speak, Cowell then sat down and decided which three to take through to the live finals. The news was broken to each contestant separately in the living room of Cowell's house. Here he summed up how he and his two female sidekicks – including his long-standing friend and ally, Sinitta – had assessed his progress. 'Vocally, I think you were terrific,' he told Brookstein, 'the girls with me absolutely adored you.' He reminded Brookstein that he hadn't looked him in the eye when he said he believed he could win. 'I have to pick somebody who I genuinely believe can be a winner,' he told him, racking up the suspense, 'and I'd like you to be in my final three.' There were no wild histrionics, Brookstein merely nodded and said, 'Oh.' If Cowell had hoped to see more belief and commitment from Brookstein at this point, he would have been disappointed. He also put Satchell and Keays through, completing his final three for the live shows.

Here we saw for the first time how far the show would go in creating friction between the judges. Walsh had often criticized Brookstein during the competition and Cowell was shown trying to stoke the flames of this argument backstage. 'Louis lives in a tunnel that wide,' he said, with his hands about five inches apart. 'He wouldn't know talent if it smacked him in the face. You know what I'd love you to do. I'd love you to go on that stage on Saturday night and shut Louis Walsh up.' Given the millions of records that Walsh and Cowell had sold with Westlife, it seems unlikely that Cowell genuinely believed Walsh 'wouldn't know talent if it smacked him in the face'. Rather, it would appear that this was a bit of mischief-making to provide more drama on the show.

It was drama that Walsh was more than happy to go along with, telling Brookstein, after his first live performance, that he reminded him of 'a cab driver who would sing cabaret at the weekend'. Osbourne, too, was critical of Brookstein, saying, 'You grin at everything! I can sit here and slag you and you just grin!' Cowell, who as Brookstein's mentor was standing next to him on stage, said, 'Louis, if you haven't got anything constructive to say, shut up!' Walsh reminded Cowell that he had 'made a career' out of being rude to contestants on television. The following week, Cowell was shown telling Brookstein, 'Forget about Sharon and Louis, because nobody takes them seriously anyway.' Sure enough, on the second live show, Walsh continued the feud by accusing Cowell of 'cheating' by allowing Brookstein to be accompanied by a choir. Osbourne asked him, 'Why try and sing like a black person? You ain't got soul!'

Once again the following week, the feud between Brookstein and Cowell's rival judges was stoked. Backstage, Cowell encouraged Brookstein to vent his feelings about Osbourne on camera, which the singer did, saying she had been in America so long that she only knew rock music and didn't understand soul. When it came time for Osbourne's verdict on the show that Saturday, she sat silent and stony-faced for several agonizing seconds. 'Oh sorry,' she snapped sarcastically, 'I thought I was back in America, I forgot I was in England.' Cowell could scarcely conceal his grin as the tension between the pair mounted. However, she and Walsh were, ultimately, enthusiastic about Brookstein that week. Could it be that news of Brookstein's high vote count each week had forced the pair to be more positive? There was a lot of love in the room. Walsh even managed to chuck a plug for the new Westlife album into his comments, much to Cowell's amusement. The peace was not to last, though. Osbourne wondered the following week if Brookstein was 'a one-trick pony' and Walsh said he was 'a little bit bored' by the song and criticized Brookstein's clothes, too. When it was Cowell's turn to comment, he smiled and said smugly, 'I always believe in giving the public what they want.' He added, 'Fashion advice from Louis Walsh? Yeah, right!'

Once more, Brookstein was voted through. He and Walsh's opera act G4 consistently avoided being in the dreaded bottom two each week and appeared to be the main contenders in the competition. Just as sparks flew between Cowell and Walsh over Brookstein, so the same happened with the critiques of G4. Thornton asked the band about their experience at gentleman's club Stringfellows during the week. Mindful of the stories about Cowell and lap dancers, Walsh joked, 'Was Simon there?' Without missing a beat, Cowell calmly told Walsh, who prefers to be private about his love life, 'You weren't there, were you, Louis?' The Irishman was duly humbled for a moment, though he did bite back, telling Cowell and Brookstein they were looking increasingly like one another. 'There's a bit of a clone thing going on here,' he quipped. 'One Simon Cowell is enough, we don't need another.' Ever ready to have the final word, Cowell told Brookstein, 'Louis has just paid you the highest compliment you've ever had – that you look like me!' In *Pop Idol*, Cowell's squabbling with Waterman was an occasional treat. On *The X Factor*, with the added spice of rivalry between mentors, the judges were at each other's throat most weeks. The conflict wasn't a bolt-on theme, but one of the major underlying premises of the show, and Cowell was at the helm.

In the semi-final, it seemed that peace had broken out again. Osbourne and Walsh complimented Brookstein on his performances, with the Irishman praising Brookstein for his confidence. However, he soon turned the praise on its head by adding, 'Simon, you're a very confident guy and your artist is becoming as confident as you. Sometimes it's not very nice.' Cowell asked Walsh what he was trying to imply. 'I think you're both overconfident,' confirmed the Irishman. Summing up, Cowell said that the point of *The X Factor*, particularly in regard to the over twenty-fives category, was to give a break to people who had 'been kicked in the teeth by the industry'. Walsh and Osbourne both interrupted angrily, shouting that Cowell should stop fishing for sympathy. When it came to the results show, Walsh's band G4 were the first act announced as going through. Would the second place be taken by Cowell's Brookstein or Osbourne's Tabby Callaghan? Tension, as ever, was running high. Cowell was later to say he felt 'aged by ten years', such was his stress. When Thornton announced Brookstein's name, Cowell's emotions exploded and he grabbed his singer in a passionate bear hug of celebration, patting him violently on the back.

'It's going to be so much fun,' said Brookstein when asked how he felt about getting through to the final, 'I'm really looking forward to it.' It was destined to be a dramatic night of mixed emotions for him. During the week building up to the final, the contest between Brookstein and G4 was hyped, as was the battle between Cowell and Walsh. Unlike on the *Idol* shows, the judges were also competitors. Walsh criticized Brookstein in the press regularly, and the singer wondered aloud whether Walsh would be quite so bold 'to his face' on the night. A press conference was called and it ran much like a weigh-in for a boxing match. 'He's a very aggravating little man,' said Brookstein of Walsh. 'Sometimes you meet people along the way you don't get on with,' he continued, 'and you just think "mug" and walk the other way.' Walsh was asked to respond and said, 'I don't care if I never see Steve again.' Inevitably it descended into a squabble between Cowell and Walsh, in which the former was in his element – his *X Factor* masterplan was proving to be the real winner before the final had even started.

During rehearsals on the evening of the final, Brookstein interrupted some praise he was receiving from Osbourne, by saying, 'Yadda, yadda, yadda.' Later, with the cameras rolling, Cowell kicked off proceedings with a provocative vow. 'By the end of the evening,' he said, 'I will wipe the smug smile of Louis Walsh's face.' After the first round of songs, both Walsh and Osbourne damned Brookstein with faint praise, the Irishman saying his performances had been 'very pleasant' and Osbourne telling him he was 'like a Volvo, very reliable'. Cowell said it was a 'ridiculous comment'. These somewhat cool exchanges were, however, merely a precursor to the fiery words that followed Brookstein's last performance of the night. During that song's introductory VT, Brookstein was shown having a heart-to-heart with his interviewer. He explained that he had kept his estate car and speakers in his garage, in case he didn't get a record deal out of the show. 'Do I keep it just in case?' he wondered aloud, and was then shown bursting into tears.

The VT came to an end. In the studio, Cowell told Thornton that Brookstein had had 'a tough time in his life, this guy, and he's had a bit of an onslaught from [Walsh and Osbourne]." Brookstein then sang 'Against All Odds'. With his 'onslaught' comment, it was as if Cowell had lit a touch-paper. He wouldn't need to wait long for the explosion. During the judges' final verdicts of the series, Brookstein faced an astonishing attack from Osbourne. 'What did you think of Steve's final song?' Thornton asked her. Someone in the audience suggested, 'Fabulous?' a favourite word of Osbourne's.

'No, not fabulous,' said Osbourne, shaking her head. 'Listen, everyone knows the way I feel about Steve; I've never been a Steve fan,' she continued. 'Steve has a very nice voice, for me he's not a superstar. I just have to say this: I am so fed up with Mr Humble, and Mr "Should I Sell My Volkswagen?"' The audience began to boo her, but this only increased her rage. 'He's overconfident,' she shouted. 'He's been overconfident since day one. He's not what he seems, believe me. All that BS that he gives out every week – he's even fooled Simon!' Cowell whispered to Brookstein not to respond. By this stage the studio was in chaos, with much of the audience booing and hissing at Osbourne, who was turning redder with anger by the second.

She wasn't finished. 'He's full of crap and he's an average singer,' she stormed. 'Ask everybody else on this contest – he's overly confident.' Cowell, with his arm resting on Brookstein's shoulder, said, 'You know what, there's an awful lot I could say… but I won't, I won't.' An audience member screamed, 'Don't stoop to her level.' Cowell continued, 'I think it was inappropriate to be personal tonight,' he said. Osbourne interrupted, 'You both know he's going to win, but the public should know he's a fake!' Cowell stormed, 'Sharon – shut up, shut up! We are very fortunate, we have careers. This means a lot to him, you should remember that.' To which Osbourne replied, 'Stop playing the victim!'

Cowell then moved backstage to await the results. When the lines were closed and the votes counted and verified, he returned to the stage alongside Brookstein. Next to them were Walsh and his act G4. Thornton announced that over eight million votes had been cast. She said, 'The winner of *The X Factor* is...' Following a lengthy delay, during which Cowell flared his nostrils with nerves, she finally shouted the winners' name: 'Steve!' If Cowell was already aware of the result, he kept it well hidden as he leapt on Brookstein, hugging and slapping him with jubilation. Cowell's grin could hardly have been wider. The first reality show he had been in charge of had come to an end with two great acts, an explosive grand final, eight million votes and him as the winning judge. He composed himself long enough to shake hands with G4 and Walsh. Then he hugged Thornton and smiled gleefully. Brookstein then sang 'Against All Odds' again and utterly fluffed it, giggling, messing up his lyrics and even interrupting the song at one point to say, 'Thank you, that's what I've got to say.'

At the song's conclusion, with tickertape raining down, Cowell joined his triumphant act on the stage. Brookstein thanked his mentor profusely. 'Simon, in that first audition, if you hadn't put me through, I wouldn't be standing *here*,' he said, thumping the stage with his foot. 'I really appreciate it,' he added, embracing Cowell. Thornton then said, 'Simon, you came here to win and you did win. How are you feeling tonight?' Back came that huge smile. 'Well,' he said, trying and failing to tone down his grin, 'I am just so thrilled for this guy. It's what this competition is all about.' He then thanked all the producers one by one and the commissioners at ITV. Despite being smug about his victory, he was also gracious and keen to share the credit. However, there was no denying who the real winner of *The X Factor* was: the winning judge, executive producer and star of the show – Simon Cowell. He had faced writs, hurdles and criticisms but had produced a smash-hit show all of his own. That night he celebrated his success and dreamed of what was to come for him, *The X Factor* and Syco.

The first thing on the horizon for Cowell was to launch Brookstein's career through his record label. Here was where he could partially judge the full extent of *The X Factor*'s success. Would – as with the *Idol* shows – the winner go on to make a fortune in record sales? Could Brookstein be the next Will Young, Gareth Gates or Kelly Clarkson? In the early stages it all went swimmingly, but soon choppier waters were to throw the plans dramatically off course. Brookstein released 'Against All Odds' in December 2004 and it reached the number one spot in January 2005. His debut covers album, *Heart & Soul*, also went to the top of the charts, selling around 200,000 copies. However, there the story between Cowell and Brookstein began to go disastrously wrong. Within three months he was dropped by Cowell's label after a series of disagreements. Cowell wanted Brookstein to release more cover versions, but Brookstein wanted to release his own material. 'I was custard pied,' he says. Brookstein then formed his own record label, and his album of self-penned tunes only made it to number 165 in the charts.

Brookstein says that it wasn't just the music he was asked to record that he disagreed on, it was also the way he was marketed as an artist. 'Simon Cowell put me into suits,' he told *The Guardian*. 'He said, "We want you to look and dress and act like a star."

I took that on board.' However, he says that Cowell also asked him to perform what he felt were demeaning tasks, including dull corporate duties, such as singing to competition winners. 'When he asked me to do stuff that wasn't befitting of a star, I thought, no, you wouldn't have Michael McDonald or any of my heroes going to Mavis on checkout five and singing,' he complained. So they went their separate ways.

Since then, Brookstein has reappeared from time to time in the media to take a swipe at Cowell and *The X Factor*. It's safe to say that relations between the two men will never be friendly again. Brookstein's angry criticisms of Cowell mean that reconciliation will never be possible. 'There is absolutely no way he would want me within a hundred miles of him,' says Brookstein. As for Cowell, when asked at a press conference about his lost relationship with Brookstein, he said simply, 'To be honest, [the show] was a little bit shallow in the talent department that year.' Brookstein's dive was a spectacular one for a man who polled five and a half million votes in the grand final of series one of *The X Factor*. He remains angry about his experience and is now said to be penning a damning book about his experiences, entitled *X Factor Nightmares: The Manipulations. The Greed. The Deceptions.* One gets the sense it isn't going to be kind to Cowell.

In the end, the runners-up, G4, fared far better than the winner. They signed to Cowell's Sony BMG label, and their debut album went double platinum, selling over 600,000 copies and going to number one. They released two further albums, the first of which went as high as number six in the charts. Their operatic take on pop classics proved to be a surprising hit. It was not a surprise to Cowell, though, who – separate to any reality television show –

had put together a not dissimilar band himself during the previous years. After hearing Andrea Bocelli and Sarah Brightman sing the Italian classical crossover song 'Con Te Partirò' in 2001, Cowell became obsessed with the idea of forming a multinational band that would combine the best elements of opera and popular music into a winning formula.

Quietly, hardly noticed by the general public despite his growing fame, he spent nearly three years searching for members to be part of his project. The four who made the cut were Spanish baritone, Carlos Marín; a pair of talented tenors, Urs Bühler from Switzerland and American David Miller, and a French pop singer, Sébastien Izambard. Together they became Il Divo – which means 'star' in Italian – and signed to Cowell's Syco label. Their vocals were as impressive as the finest opera singers, but their looks were a million miles away from the portly Three Tenors. None of Il Divo would look out of place on the cover of GQ magazine. Their first, eponymous album was a combination of operatic covers of classic songs (including Frank Sinatra's 'My Way' and Toni Braxton's 'Unbreak My Heart') and original tracks such as 'Mama'. It gave Cowell another number one album in the UK, and his thirst for international success was quenched when ultimately it went to the number one spot in thirteen countries and the top five in many more. For Cowell, the success of Il Divo – and of *The X Factor*'s operatic pop act G4 – made up for the disappointment of the show's winner Steve Brookstein.

Cowell is not a man who gives up easily, so despite his dismay at Brookstein's post-*X Factor* career, he marched on to the next series full of confidence that they could not just produce another entertaining show, but crown a champion worthy of the name.

At the outset of series two, all three judges insisted they wouldn't repeat the attention-grabbing dramatics of the first series. 'We won't let our egos get in the way of the contestants,' said Cowell, who was backed up by his fellow judges in this. 'The slate has been wiped clean,' added Walsh, while Osbourne said, 'It's not about us, it's about them, the contestants, and that's where the focus should be.' Fine words, but in reality it wouldn't take long for the judges to start bickering.

It took even less time for them to start damning the early auditionees. A female duo from Wales called Total Eclipse sang 'Summer Of 69'. Cowell told the first member that she reminded him of *Little Britain* character Vicky Pollard, then he went on to tell the second member that she resembled 'a stretched version' of her band-mate. 'So I look like a man?' asked the first member, clearly offended. Cowell was in no mood to compromise and replied, 'You don't look like a man, you look like a man dressed as a woman.' They stormed out, but the 'stretched version' member wasn't entirely put off by Cowell's rudeness. 'I'd still do him,' she said afterwards.

Another controversial audition came from Chico Slimani, who was told by Cowell, 'That was the corniest audition I've ever seen in my life.' However, against Cowell's strongest urging, Walsh and Osbourne voted him through. Cowell was furious; he stood up and said to Chico, 'No offence,' then he turned to Walsh and shouted, 'but you're pathetic.' He then approached a producer and said, 'I want a word with you – come on!' He moved the producer into a corridor and told a cameraman, 'Don't film this,' as he shut the door. He was later filmed, in the distance, telling Walsh, 'You are making a fool out of yourself, and you're making a fool out of the competition. Louis, I'm telling you as a friend, you've got to stop doing this.' Contrived drama or genuine rows? Either way, it made for entertaining television.

There were plenty more amusing moments for Cowell. An eighty-three-year-old woman called Dorothy Morrison told him at her audition that he was her 'hero', to which he grinned and told her she was a 'saucy little thing'. When fifty-nine-year-old supermarket worker Beulah was voted out, Walsh jokingly said that he would have given her a chance. Cowell called his bluff by handing the singer a piece of paper with Walsh's mobile phone number on it. Any doubts as to whether Cowell had given her the real number evaporated when she dialled it from the corridor and Walsh's phone rang. This wasn't the first time Cowell had performed such a prank. In series two of *Pop Idol* he gave out fellow judge Pete Waterman's mobile phone number live on air.

When it came time for the judges to be awarded their respective categories, Cowell was less than pleased to be handed the groups. Despite his annoyance, it served him well to be handed a category he was openly not keen on, as it lessened suspicions that, as executive producer, he was in any way abusing his position in terms of the competition. He showed an unconventional approach with the bands during the boot-camp phase of the show. While Walsh and Osbourne worked their categories hard, Cowell treated the bands to a good old-fashioned boozing session one night, and the following morning he told them, 'Impress me. There's no excuses today. You've got good songs.' Perhaps the finest band to emerge from the pack at this stage was Journey South, which comprised brothers Andy and Carl Pemberton from Middlesbrough. Their story chimed with Cowell as much as their music did. Having worked hard to build a musical career, they had been forced to move back home when they built up debts that reached into five figures. Yet here they were, giving it a second go, hoping to make it. No wonder Cowell related to them. Sure enough, they were one of the bands to make it to the live finals – but only after Cowell had whisked his acts off to his holiday home in Spain.

Walsh had taken his acts to his Dublin home. There he put through three acts, including Shayne Ward. One of the acts he sent home at this stage was a young Londoner called Alexandra Burke. It was not the last that the show would hear of her.

In the run-up to the live finals, Cowell faced public criticism of his mentoring skills from fellow judge Walsh. The Irishman claimed Cowell – who was combining filming series four of *American Idol* and *The X Factor*, flying between Britain and America to do so – wasn't spending enough time with his acts. 'That's a bit late, isn't it?' he said, when he learned that Cowell was only arriving back in Britain on the Thursday before the first live show. 'I have been working with my acts for three weeks now and I often text them and chat on the phone. Sharon flew into the country last week to be with hers. It looks like Simon only has a couple of days to get things right.' Cowell was enjoying a hectic but pleasing schedule. Not only was he criss-crossing the Atlantic to film two shows, his and Walsh's band Westlife had just had their fifth number one album success with *Face to Face*.

Walsh had more reason to giggle when the live finals started less than ideally for Cowell the mentor, who lost an act in each of the first two weeks. However, for Cowell the producer all was well. Manchester guy Shayne Ward, a singer in Walsh's category, was proving to be the frontrunner of the series. With his sweet pop voice and boy-band looks, he quickly picked up plenty of support. There was – despite promises to the contrary at the outset of series two – drama between the judges, not least in week five of the finals. Walsh offended Osbourne and the fiery female judge threw a glass of water over the Irishman. As she drenched Walsh, Cowell's smiling approval in the background was clear for all to see. He, too, upset Walsh around about this time. During an appearance on ITV's *This Morning* show, Cowell was asked if he could ever replace Walsh as a judge. 'It would be difficult to find someone that stupid,' he replied.

The week after he was drenched by Osbourne, Walsh was upset again when his act Nicholas was voted out by his fellow judges. He fumed, saying that Cowell and Osbourne had 'humiliated him', then he walked out of the studio, vowing never to return. He had a successful career regardless of the show, he told friends, and he wasn't willing to be Cowell's 'puppet'. During the following week, Walsh also spoke to the *Daily Mirror*. 'It's been a week from hell,' he said. 'I was seriously considering never coming back. I've had sleepless nights. I'm actually taking sleeping tablets to get some rest. I want assurances from the producers they will not humiliate me any more or I won't hesitate to walk again. It's in their hands.' Cowell told Walsh he was sorry, but was in no mood to beg Walsh to return. He said, 'It's very simple. I've apologised to Louis. If he turns up, he turns up. If he doesn't, he doesn't. I'm now focusing on the contestants, as we all should. They are the most important part of the show.'

Many viewers took these words with a pinch of salt, but happily Walsh did return the following week. He had the favourite, Ward, in his category, so it never seemed likely he would quit the show, and with it the chance of a stake in Ward's glory. Cowell managed to deliver a withering put-down when he was asked on ITV2's *The Xtra Factor* how he thought Walsh's return show had gone. 'Oh, I thought Louis played an absolute blinder,' he sighed, his sarcasm clear for all to see.

There was another twist that evening when Cowell voted out his own act, The Conway Sisters, in favour of his nemesis, Slimani. Not that this was enough to get the singer into the final, which ended up being contested by three acts: Shayne Ward, Andy Abraham and Journey South. This was the first time a reality show included three acts in the final, but the mathematics of it wasn't hard to understand: three acts equals three fan-bases equals extra phone votes equals extra revenue.

On the night, however, it was all about Ward. Cowell told him after he sang 'If You're Not The One': 'By any standard outside of a show like this, that was, in my opinion, absolutely flawless.' With Journey South already voted out, Cowell was able to lay on his praise of Ward. 'I think this competition has genuinely found a star.' He smiled. 'And in my opinion you have the X Factor.' Ward was indeed voted the winner and sang 'That's My Goal' like a true champion. The first final had been tainted by Osbourne's tantrum at Brookstein and his chaotic performance of the winners' single. As Cowell watched Ward sing, he felt as if the show had, second time round, got closer to the sort of perfection he craves from every project he works on. The Christmas of 2005 saw Cowell enjoying enormous success in the charts. Ward enjoyed a Christmas number one with his winner's single, and Cowell's band Il Divo were also top of the charts in several countries with their album *The Christmas Collection*.

With the success of *The X Factor*, Cowell's profile was raised ever higher, and with the upside of such increased celebrity came an inevitable downside. In July 2006, Cowell awoke to some very uncomfortable morning headlines. 'Exclusive: The Sex Factor', screamed the front page of the *Daily Mirror*. Alongside the headline was a photograph of Cowell peering round the front door of his London home, immediately after an attractive, thin lady had left the house. The first paragraph of the story said, 'Simon Cowell has been cheating on girlfriend Terri Seymour for six months, it emerged yesterday.' Cowell strongly denies this claim and says that he had been meeting Jasmine Lennard to discuss television projects.

The story claimed that Cowell had first met the leggy lady in January in a restaurant. But who was she? Jasmine Lennard's father made a fortune through his Sacha retail shoe empire and her mother was a Bond girl. As for Lennard herself, she had a small role in the Guy Ritchie movie *Revolver* and had appeared on reality television shows *Make Me a Supermodel* and *Trust Me: I'm a Holiday Rep*, where she was infamous for making bitchy remarks to the other participants. When confronted about her outspoken nature, she had used Cowell as a reference point, saying, 'I was given this bitch label. If it's making Simon Cowell millions, I don't mind. People started to know who I was.'

Plenty more people certainly knew who she was after the *Mirror* story claiming Cowell was having an affair with her. Both parties quickly issued denials. Lennard said, 'It wasn't what it looked like. Simon is a good friend; we were discussing work. We have been friends for some time.' As for Cowell, he said, 'These stories come out, but Jasmine is just a friend. There were other people at the house too. Terri has absolutely nothing to worry about.' As speculation mounted, the *Daily Mail* reproduced one of Cowell's quotes from a few years earlier. Asked if he was a faithful partner, he had said, 'Well, I am a bit of a flirt, but I'm pretty good. My eyes do wander, and daily. It's what you do after those eyes that counts.'

Despite the strong denials of wrongdoing, when Seymour arrived back in Britain, she and Cowell had a very public showdown. Cowell went to meet her at Heathrow Airport and she was reportedly furious with him when she arrived, refusing to kiss him and calling him a 'silly little man'. He is on the record as saying that since meeting Seymour he has been shouted at like never before in his life. Cowell ushered her into a Starbucks café to try and avoid their heated discussion becoming too public. An onlooker, quoted in the *Mirror*, said, 'Judging by the look on his face, I'd say he was getting it with both barrels. Their body language said it all. She refused to kiss him when he greeted her and they only touched for a little hug.

'She shouted that he was "a silly little man". He pulled her into a quiet corner as she waited for a coffee. He was aware people recognized him and was talking very quietly. It looked like he was begging for another chance as she vented her fury. She was gesticulating a lot and it didn't look like a friendly chat. As soon as they saw the cameras it was all forced smiles, but even then they didn't get within three feet of each other.' Afterwards Cowell loaded Seymour's bags into his brand-new Rolls-Royce and drove the pair to his Holland Park mansion where they sipped champagne in the garden. Seymour stayed the night. She emerged smiling the following morning and assured waiting reporters that she and Cowell were still an item. He backed this up, saying, 'Terri and me are absolutely fine. We've spoken and we're fine.'

Seymour's mother, Margaret, also insisted that all was well between Cowell and her daughter. 'Simon likes her very much,' she told the *Mirror*. 'We've met him lots of times and you can see he cares for her. She knows what he's like. She's knows he's rich and famous, she knows women throw themselves at him and that he likes it, but she trusts him. They trust each other. Simon wouldn't be so stupid. If he was going to cheat, he would do it at a hotel, anywhere, but not at his own house for anyone to see.'

Meanwhile, Cowell was continuing to have success with his acts, including Westlife, who were preparing to release their eighth album, consisting entirely of covers. Its name? *The Love Album*. It went straight to number one, and was quickly followed by another Cowell top-spot album, *Siempre* by Il Divo, which included a cover of Bryan Adams's 'Have You Ever Really Loved A Woman'? Given the success of Il Divo, Cowell quickly followed up with a children's version of the band called Angelis. After nationwide auditions, the six-piece band was completed, comprising kids between the ages of eleven and fourteen. Their first eponymous album was released in July 2006 in the same month as *The Love Album* and *Siempre*, reaching number two. It was a successful few weeks for Cowell in the pop charts.

The Lennard story refused to go away, though, not least because Lennard has continued to speak about Cowell. Talking in July 2007, a year after the claims of her affair with Cowell first broke, she said, 'I adore him'. Lennard continued, 'I have a lot of respect for Simon. Everything he says is golden because he has so much experience.' She has the initials 'SC' tattooed onto her arm, but is coy when asked whether they refer to Cowell. 'It's someone important to me and I'm happy to have the tattoo there for the rest of my life,' she said. 'I'm seeing someone but can't talk about it.'

This sort of feverish media speculation about his love life was something Cowell was becoming increasingly familiar with. Already a famous man, his star was rising ever higher...

# CHAPTER SEVEN

# VILLAIN TURNED HERO

When he first came to the public's attention through *Pop Idol* in 2001, Cowell's stature could best be described as infamous. He was Mr Nasty, the man we loved to hate. In 2003, for instance, he had appeared at number thirty-three in Channel 4's list of the all-time one hundred worst Britons. As the *Sunday Express* said at the time, 'Cowell is annoying, smug, snide, rude, vain, mean and prancing, with strange hair and a twisted smile.' However, as the level of international recognition increased during the decade, he managed to alter his position from infamy to fame. Along the way, he became, if not the man everyone loved to love, a man who we respect.

With the assistance and guidance of Clifford, Cowell was widely interviewed and profiled in national newspapers, where the man who has always been quick to offer judgments put himself on the line to be assessed by others. His charm worked wonders on most of the journalists he encountered. Jaci Stephen of the *Mail on Sunday* wrote, 'All men to whom women are instantly drawn have one thing in common: they listen to you as if you are the only person in the room, and heaven knows, Cowell does. He is charismatic, articulate, bright and funny.' It wasn't just female journalists he charmed: 'He's funny, he's charming and he's quite good-looking,' wrote Ian Hyland in the *Sunday Mirror*. 'He's got twinkly eyes and he's very charismatic.' The broadsheets, too, wrote approvingly about this icon of pop culture. A profiler from *The Independent* said, 'A good celebrity is someone who knows they have a ridiculous job. They understand that being a celebrity is actually stupid and have fun with it. Simon Cowell, for example, I think has a lot fun being Simon Cowell.'

Part of being Simon Cowell involves working with charities and other good causes. He has appeared on two advertisements for the organization People for the Ethical Treatment of Animals (PETA). The first, launched in January 2005, saw him front a new anti-fur campaign. He was pictured cuddling a dog, with an accompanying quote, saying, 'If you wouldn't wear your dog, please don't wear any fur.' A PETA spokesman told reporters, 'We're thrilled to have Simon on board. This advert brings home the reality that... the fur trade means animals have been cruelly trapped or beaten to death.' While there is no doubt that Cowell, a celebrated animal lover, took part in this campaign for sincere reasons, it didn't harm his image either: 'Cowell Shows His Soft Side,' ran the headline on the *Sky Showbiz* website.

The following year Cowell was back for more as he fronted a second PETA campaign to educate people about the lethal dangers of leaving dogs in cars during warm weather. 'Far be it from me to be critical, but I find it really appalling that, this year, thousands of dogs will die of heatstroke inside parked cars,' said Cowell, as he petted a dog called Claude. 'Never ever leave your dog inside a parked car. Your dog idolizes you. In warm weather, keep him safe at home.' In an interview on the PETA website, he expanded further. He was asked if he would be more sympathetic to a reality show contestant if he knew that he or she was an animal lover. 'Yes, I mean, of course,' he said. 'Maybe some people are surprised that I like animals, but there's a bit of a difference between telling someone who's a useless singer, "You're a useless singer," and drowning a puppy. I once had an incident with a guy who auditioned who actually admitted he likes killing animals. He didn't go through.'

PETA has campaigned against cruelty in the horse-racing industry, but interestingly, in the same year as Cowell made his fur advertisement for the group, he also became a partner at the Royal Ascot Racing Club and became part of a syndicate that owned Motivator, the six-million-pound colt that won the 2005 Epsom Derby. He even has his own box at Ascot. His colleague and friend Piers Morgan, the former *Daily Mirror* editor, spent a day there with Cowell and other guests in 2008. Morgan lost £1,000 through his day's gambling while Cowell made £5,000. 'Oops...' he told Morgan, 'looks like I got lucky again.' All Morgan could do to console himself was recall the famous maxim: the better the gambler, the worse the man.

In the sixth season of *American Idol*, two episodes of the live finals were devoted to raising money for charity. The combined brainchild of Simon Fuller and British filmmaker and Comic Relief founder Richard Curtis, *Idol Gives Back* saw funds donated to charities for every vote cast. In the run-up to the show, Cowell and *Idol* host Seacrest visited disadvantaged children in Africa. 'I think the thing that probably affected us the most was how nice the people were,' said Cowell in a promotional video for the *Idol Gives Back* show. 'We were hanging out with these kids – you know, four years old, six years old, eight years old – who work on a rubbish tip... Terrible conditions. But they were just sweet, nice little kids. And at the point where we actually took them somewhere nice, it was how polite and thankful they were [that struck me]. That's probably what affected me the most.' *Idol Gives Back* returned for the seventh season, but was dropped for the eighth due to the economic crisis.

British children's hospices have also benefitted from Cowell's time and energy. One such institution is The Chase hospice in Artington, Guildford. Cowell's role there was secret for many years, until Max Clifford revealed it during Cowell's second *This is Your Life* episode. 'He probably won't thank me for saying it, but in the six or seven years since we first met up, Simon has done an awful lot of things for an awful lot of people that no one knows anything about. The Chase is a wonderful children's hospice where everything is done to make things as good as possible for as long as possible. Every single time [*The X Factor*] goes on air, children from that hospice and other hospices from all over the country go to every show; they're Simon's guests. They go backstage and meet Simon, he introduces them to everyone else and he makes a real fuss of them. More than that, he's become an uncle to many of the kids at The Chase. They phone him and they talk to him. He visits The Chase regularly with Terri. What he's done for The Chase and a lot of the children there, year in, year out, nobody knows about. They do, I do, and the families do, and it's to his eternal credit.' Cowell had appeared somewhat uncomfortable throughout Clifford's eulogy. Coming as it did from his press advisor, the praise didn't seem as spontaneous as it might have had it come from somebody who worked at The Chase, but all the same, it was an opportunity to see his caring side.

Another part of Clifford's job was to advise Cowell how to deal with the regular rumours that he is gay. Speculation about Cowell's sexuality became more rampant the more famous he became, despite his high-profile relationship with Terri Seymour. Could the bitchy, vain and gentle-voiced Cowell really be heterosexual, asked the gossipers. It was speculation that the man himself dismissed, though he understood its origin. 'I don't play rugby, I don't drink beer, I don't hang out in pubs, I take an interest in what I wear,' he said in *I Hate to Be Rude, But...*, 'but if I were gay, I would happily admit it. I'm not gay, but if I didn't know me and I met me I probably would think, "Yeah, he's gay."' It was a convincing response, but it wouldn't be the last time he was asked to respond to questions about his sexuality. As we've seen, the idealistic image he has of his parents' marriage continues to cast a shadow over his own romantic adventures, and his lack of interest in having children has proved to be another obstacle to sustaining romantic happiness for him.

Even with *The X Factor* and *American Idol* going strong, Cowell still wasn't satisfied by the fame and fortune the two shows were bringing him. As competitive and ambitious as ever, he wanted to take his television career to even higher levels. During 2006 and 2007 the airwaves of Britain and America were flooded by a tidal wave of new programmes that Cowell was involved in, either on or off screen, or both. In the process, Cowell confirmed his progress from a reality-show judge to television genius with a stranglehold on TV's light entertainment genre. If you lived in Britain and America, watched television and enjoyed those programmes, you will almost certainly have watched at least one Cowell programme in recent years.

First out of the traps was *American Inventor*, for which he joined forces with another straight-talking British reality TV star, Peter Jones. With an estimated net worth of £157 million, made mainly from the telecommunications trade, Jones is a business sensation who's best known in the UK for his role on the BBC show *Dragons' Den*, in which members of the public pitch business ideas to Jones and other entrepreneurs, in the hope that they will invest in their business venture in return for a slice of equity. Jones came up with an idea for a new show called *The Inventor* and took it to Cowell. The pair then sold it to the ABC network and it premiered on the channel with a two-hour special on 16 March 2006, with Cowell remaining behind the scenes as co-producer. It was an immediate hit, becoming the number-one show on the network. The production duties and subsequent riches were divided between Fremantle North America, Peter Jones Television and Syco.

Just five months later, another Cowell television show hit the American airwaves with a two-hour premiere. The original plan was to launch a show on ITV called *Star Duets*, which would be a talent show in which famous people would be paired with a professional singer in a weekly competition. However, the BBC beat him to the post, announcing a similar show called *Just the Two of Us*. Cowell considered taking legal action, though as ever he was honest and philosophical. He said, 'I don't know if we are going to sue yet. We will have to wait and see exactly how close it is to ours before we make out mind up. This sort of thing happens all the time in television; it's all about who gets there first with an idea.'

Ultimately, Cowell decided to sell his concept to America instead and found a willing home for the programme – now called *Celebrity Duets* – at Fox, the home of *American Idol*. After weeks of teaser advertisements, on 29 August 2006, the show debuted there with American singer, actor and television personality Wayne Brady as the host, and a judging panel comprising rock royalty Little Richard, legendary producer David Foster and singer Marie Osmond. Cowell once more stayed behind the scenes as executive producer, in which role he attracted a galaxy of stars to take part as singers, including Dionne Warwick, Gladys Knight and Smokey Robinson. It proved a success, but the next show up Cowell's sleeve was to become even more successful.

The idea for the show had come to Cowell the previous year. In 2005, he developed a new concept with his long-time colleague Ken Warwick, who worked as producer and director on both *Pop Idol* and *American Idol*. For this show, he referred back to one of his favourite childhood programmes, *New Faces*, which in turn was influenced by the granddaddy of all television talent contests, *Opportunity Knocks*. First broadcast on radio in the 1940s, *Opportunity Knocks* moved to television in 1956, and reappeared periodically on our screens until the 1990s. America had had it's own version of the show, too – *Major Bowes' Amateur Hour* – which was first broadcast on radio in the 1930s. There the host, Bowes, would sound a bell or hit a gong when he had tired of a contestant.

It was a popular show, but one that had – according to many – fallen out of fashion. However, following his guiding principle of knowing what the public want before they do and then giving it to them, Cowell and Warwick decided to revive the genre with a show of their own. Presented by successful, BAFTA-award-winning chat-show host Paul O'Grady, the programme would be called *Paul O'Grady's Got Talent*, and would be sold to ITV. It was due to pilot in September 2005, with a view to rolling out the *Got Talent* franchise internationally. However, in March 2006, O'Grady defected from ITV to Channel 4, leaving Cowell without a host. It seemed that once again Cowell's idea had fallen flat before being able to sell it to ITV. However, rather than sulk or search for a new man to front the show in the UK, Cowell decided to launch the *Got Talent* concept in America.

In the US, Cowell sold the show to the prestigious NBC channel, and in June 2006, the audition tour for *America's Got Talent* began. He couldn't appear on the show personally, though, due to the terms of his *American Idol* contract with Fox, and in any case, his commitments on *Idol* and *The X Factor* didn't leave him much spare time.

The judging panel he put together for the first series raised a lot of eyebrows. Cowell and *Knight Rider/Baywatch* star David Hasselhoff had first crossed paths many years earlier, in the early 1990s when BMG asked Cowell to replicate Hasselhoff's German pop success in Britain. It was a trick Cowell found hard to pull off, due in part to Hasselhoff's eccentric personality. The actor made a fool of himself in the first UK press interview set up for him, forcing Cowell to charm and beg the journalist into not writing up the encounter. Cowell then linked Hasselhoff up with Pete Waterman to provide him with a hit, but the producer threw in the towel weeks later, complaining about the actor's unreasonable demands. Hasselhoff would not be bowed, though, and loudly burst into song in front of Cowell during a dinner at a posh hotel restaurant. Eventually Cowell managed to drag one hit out of Hasselhoff with the song 'If Only I Could Say Goodbye'. He found the experience draining and took great delight in telling Hasselhoff that he was 'precious' at their final meeting. It was the sort of talk a star such as Hasselhoff wasn't used to hearing. However, after initially being shocked by Cowell's directness, he laughed and agreed that it was true. All the same, it was time for the pair to say goodbye, and when, twelve years later, Cowell and Hasselhoff were reunited, it was proof that neither bore a grudge.

Another judge was Brandy Norwood, a glamorous singer-songwriter, music and film producer and actress, but the third judge was a rather surprising choice. British journalist Piers Morgan enjoyed a meteoric rise in his newspaper career, becoming the editor of the mighty *News of the World* at the tender age of twenty-eight in 1994. The following year he moved to become editor of the *Mirror*, where he was a controversial figure. During the Euro '96 football tournament, on the day before England played Germany, he ran the headline 'Achtung! Surrender' on the cover. He also had a court clash with Naomi Campbell and claimed the then Prime Minister's wife Cherie Blair was trying to get him fired – a claim Mrs Blair denies. After the September 11 attacks, he refocused the *Mirror* on more serious coverage, and it was here that his downfall occurred. He published photographs allegedly showing Iraqi prisoners being abused by British soldiers, but within days the photographs were exposed as fakes and Morgan was forced to resign. The *Mirror* apologized on its front page, with a headline in huge type reading, 'Sorry: We Were Hoaxed.'

In parallel with his newspaper career, Morgan had also been working as a television presenter. In 2003 he fronted a three-part BBC series called *The Importance Of Being Famous*, then he co-hosted a show on Channel 4 with journalist and political advisor Amanda Platell, called *Morgan & Platell*, which was dropped after disappointing viewing figures. So when Cowell plucked Morgan out of the career doldrums and said he was going to make him a major American television star, it was a cause of much surprise. The fact that Cowell's plan to launch Morgan in America worked so well, however, was an even bigger shock. Last but not least they needed a presenter, and Cowell hired Regis Philbin, who had been an American television star since the 1950s, to host the first series.

The show gripped America. After pre-recorded open auditions in Los Angeles, New York, Chicago, and Atlanta, in which the three judges pressed a buzzer when they were tired of an act, the show moved to live semi-finals. The field was then reduced down for a live final, which was split over two nights, as with *American Idol*, where the public would vote for the winner of the show. Once crowned, that winner would be handed the million-dollar prize and would be one of the most famous people in the country. During filming, Morgan became the 'Cowell' of the panel, comfortably taking on the role of the English villain by offering harsh put-downs. When Marlon Reynolds sang 'I Left My Heart in San Francisco', Morgan interrupted and told him, 'Maybe you should have left your voice in San Francisco, too.'

As filming proceeded, Morgan learned just what a professional Cowell was. During breaks in filming, executive producer Cowell would pace up to the judges' table and tell them they had to step their performances up a gear.

The show was an enormous success right up to and including crowning its first winner, Bianca Ryan. Premiering the same month as *Celebrity Duets*, it confirmed Cowell's pre-eminence on American television. No longer could he be considered the token Englishman, wheeled in to provide some tough talk on *Idol*, now he dominated American viewing. His choice of Morgan as a judge was proving to be an inspired one, too, as Stateside viewers had taken Morgan to their hearts, and he quickly became a celebrity in his own right, appearing on the celebrity edition of *The Apprentice*, fronted in the States by billionaire Donald Trump. Some would judge Cowell's breaking of Morgan into America as one of his most impressive achievements. It's an accomplishment that Cowell humorously referred to in a text message, when he called Morgan his 'Frankenstein' after the fictional doctor who created a monster and inflicted it on the world.

As *America's Got Talent* was hitting the American airwaves, Cowell's appearance on *Desert Island Discs* was broadcast on British radio. As a Radio 4 institution, an invitation from *Desert Island Discs* is an honour for anyone and confirmation of their high standing in the public eye. Cowell was interviewed by presenter Sue Lawley about which songs he would chose to take to a desert island with him. The young Cowell might have been surprised by his older self's choices. As a child in Elstree he had hidden and scratched his mother's big-band records, yet his choices on *Desert Island Discs* included 'Mack the Knife' by Bobby Darin – 'the best song ever made, ever produced, ever sung' – 'Summer Wind' by Frank Sinatra, 'Mr Bojangles' by Sammy Davis Jnr and 'This Guy's In Love With You' by Herb Alpert – 'the sexiest song ever'.

The inclusion of 'Unchained Melody' by the Righteous Brothers was a surprise to nobody, as Cowell has long championed the song – with which he had a hit with Robson and Jerome – as one of his favourite ever tunes. The choice of Daniel Bedingfield's 'If You're Not the One' might have been unforeseen, though. He was asked what book he would take with him, and given his down-to-earth tastes in life, *Hollywood Wives* by Jackie Collins seemed an entirely apt selection. Finally, as always on *Desert Island Discs*, the guest was asked what luxury he would take with him. The ever vain and witty Cowell chose a mirror, so he could continue to admire himself on his desert island.

Cowell appeared as a guest on high-profile television shows on both sides of the Atlantic. In England he was invited to appear on chat shows including *Friday Night With Jonathan Ross*, where the host resurrected the joke about Cowell's high-waisted trousers, and *The Frank Skinner Show*. He has also enjoyed multiple appearances on the BBC motoring programme *Top Gear*, where he was interviewed by that other television 'baddie', Jeremy Clarkson. When the host said he would offer even more extreme judgements to talent show contestants than Cowell does, his guest said, 'Well, the difference is I actually know something about music – you don't.' Clarkson countered that 'on the evidence we've seen so far' he believed Cowell 'didn't know a thing!' But Cowell remained loyal to Will Young when Clarkson attempted to draw him into banter over the singer's large jaw.

The pair then turned to discussion about cars, with both

agreeing that the Aston Martin DB7 is the most attractive car. Cowell was then shown a progression of different cars and asked to give a talent-show-style verdict on each. He called the Chrysler PT Cruiser 'a hearse', of the Fiat Multipla he said 'it's like a car with a disease – it's like it's deformed', the BMW 745i: 'They're horrible; they should fire the designer.' He then refused to take the bait and abuse traffic wardens. 'If you live in London, you need them,' he said. However, he walked straight into a trap when, with Clarkson's encouragement, he criticized bus lanes. 'That's right,' said the host, 'I don't get why the poor need to get where they're going more than you.' However, Cowell had his revenge a few minutes later when he told his host, 'You are not on TV because of the way you look.' He had held his own with alpha-male Clarkson, confirming Simon Hattenstone's assessment of Cowell in *The Guardian*: 'Cowell is both defiantly laddish and magnificently queeny... [he is] Dale Winton and Priapus.' On his second visit to *Top Gear* he was just as entertaining. Clarkson asked him whether he could become a judge on *The X Factor*. 'Shall I tell you why you couldn't?' said Cowell. 'It's because I'm ageing quite well and you're not. I was reading a review you wrote of the Jaguar the other day, and you wrote that it needs to be updated. You're the equivalent of a Jaguar who needs help.'

He has in recent years owned two £400,000 Rolls-Royce Phantoms – one in the UK, one in America – both of which are rumoured to be bullet-proof, a Range Rover, a Jaguar XKR, an Aston Martin DB9 convertible and a Mini Cooper. He has also driven an Audi R8 and Lamborghini Gallardo Spyder. In October 2007 he added a £750,000 Bugatti Veyron to the collection. It was then the fastest street-legal car, with a top speed of 253.81 miles per hour. He is proud of his car collections: 'It's completely over the top,' he said on contactmusic.com. 'I absolutely love them. I could have a hundred cars and I'd still want more. I love staring at them. I love driving them too.'

Thanks to the pranksters behind MTV practical joke show *Punk'd*, Cowell was hilariously led to believe that one of his Rolls-Royces had been stolen while he was in a meeting in Los Angeles, while his actual car was swapped for a duplicate. Not knowing he was being secretly filmed, he reacted with horror when he saw 'his' car 'stolen'. 'That's my Rolls,' he said. The actor playing the part of the valet stoked Cowell's frustration further by saying, 'How do I know it was your car?' When the police arrive, the valet continually tells them that Cowell is an 'Aussie'. The police then pretend to have received a radio report that Cowell's car has been involved in a collision on Sunset Boulevard. Cowell gulps back his upset at this news and the police eventually come clean, saying, 'We have status on the car, sir. The status is – you've just been punk'd.' It took a few seconds for the news to sink in, at which point Cowell burst out laughing. 'Oh I've been so stitched up here.' He smiled grudgingly. A source close to Cowell was widely quoted afterwards, saying Cowell had vowed vengeance on *Punk'd* host Ashton Kutcher: 'Simon fell for it one hundred per cent. He's fuming and plotting his revenge.'

Cars are not Cowell's only luxury. When asked whether he ever felt guilty about his vast financial fortune, he claimed, 'I don't have any conscience about this at all.' Probably because he's far too busy spending his money. He will happily spend thousands of pounds on Giorgio Armani T-shirts and posh French Bertulli shoes. One of his favourite clothing stores is Emporio Armani on Rodeo Drive, a three-block-long stretch of ultra-fasionable boutiques in Beverly Hills, Los Angeles. His clothes-purchasing principle is clear: if he likes an item of clothing, he buys five of them.

All that shopping can make a man hungry, and Cowell enjoys dining at celebrity restaurants, not so much for the sophisticated food as the celebrity atmosphere. Among his favourite haunts in the UK and America are The Ivy, Mr Chow, the Wolseley, and Cipriani in Mayfair. He also thinks nothing of spending small fortunes on renovating his homes. For instance, in 2008 he splashed out an estimated £50,000 on replacing the conservatory of his Holland Park home with a glass-walled room. A builder who worked on the project told the *Evening Standard*, 'It's the most ostentatious display of wealth I've ever been asked to work on.' He has also arranged substantial changes to his office at BMG headquarters.

With his hectic filming schedule on both sides of the Atlantic, Cowell spends a lot of time in the air. For instance, during the live show leg of *The X Factor* in Britain, the early auditions of *American Idol* are often being filmed across the pond, meaning Cowell has to criss-cross between the two continents. It's a hectic time for him, and all this travel is perhaps the reason why he has occasionally got contestants' names wrong during his *X Factor* live-show critiques. Still, he can console himself with the fact that he only flies by private jet. 'The champagne's better and you can smoke, which is a rare guilty pleasure at thirty-six-thousand feet these days,' he said. *X Factor* contestant Niki Evans says that despite the hectic travelling, Cowell 'always looks as fresh as daisies when he arrives... I don't know how he does it.'

Another MTV show he appeared on was *Cribs*, in which celebrities show a camera crew round their home. Cowell showed them round his Beverly Hills mansion, making a point of showing them the English products in his fridge, including HP Sauce, rice pudding and a pack of Cadbury's Flakes. His favourite drink, he said, was the almond liqueur Amaretto: 'The most delicious drink in the world,' he said, smiling, adding that he also drinks Jack Daniel's, 'because it's so butch'. Cowell enjoys a drink on the right occasions, but is rarely drunk and tends not to drink until the evening. Despite his vast riches and Hollywood lifestyle, his food tastes have always been down-to-earth. He enjoys homely, childlike dishes like fish fingers and chips, spaghetti hoops on toast, baked beans and Marks & Spencer chicken pies. An amusing moment on *Cribs* came when Cowell showed the camera crew his balcony. 'I like to recite poetry here,' he joked.

The third series of *X Factor* ended with the crowning of an artist with mammoth potential. First, though, there was the usual drama of the show, with Cowell as always in the centre of it. Brian and Craig MacDonald from Ayr in Scotland auditioned as a two-piece band called The MacDonald Brothers. The Scottish siblings had played music together since early childhood and more recently had become a full-time wedding band. At their first audition in Glasgow they sang 'Don't Worry Baby' and 'As Long As You Love Me'. They made it through boot camp and onto the live shows, where they sang 'Three Times A Lady' in the first week. From that performance on, though, they faced a tidal wave of negative feedback from Cowell each week.

For instance, in week two he told them, 'Guys, let me preface this by saying I think you are two very nice guys – we've got to know each other. But, I thought it was absolutely terrible,' he said as the audience booed and Walsh and Osbourne shook their heads in disagreement. 'I did, I did,' Cowell continued. 'It was verging on insane, that performance. After a performance like that there is not a cat in hell's chance of you winning this competition.' In response to booing from the crowd, Cowell said, 'Even the boos are low. It's just not good enough, guys. I mean it really isn't. I thought the choice of song was wrong, the guitar was wrong.'

Soon, Cowell's feedback to The MacDonald Brothers became one of the most anticipated moments of the show, with Cowell and Walsh exchanging anticipatory smiles during the brothers' performances. After they sang 'Can't Take My Eyes Off You', he said, 'In the real world, it's as good as a couple of guys standing up at the karaoke at Pontins and singing a popular song. What we're not seeing is potential star quality, but I have a horrible feeling the song is going to carry you through.' Walsh retorted by reminding Cowell that he had put Robson and Jerome into the pop market. After the brothers sang 'Love Is All Around', Cowell told them, 'That is one of the most boring songs of all time. Within the context of this show, now, it was utterly pointless.' By this point there were accusations that Cowell was anti-Scottish, so he revealed on the show that he was 'Fifty per cent Scottish – my mother's maiden name was Dalglish'. The following week he summed up their delivery of 'When You Say Nothing At All' as 'Dreary – nothing more to say'.

Craig MacDonald reveals that despite Cowell's harsh words to them on camera, they believe it wasn't a dislike of them that motivated him, but a hunger for higher phone-vote revenue. 'We learned from him just how much competition is out there and we got our first taste of how tough the music/record industry can be at that level,' says Craig. 'We were slated week after week by Simon Cowell, and although he may not have liked what we did on the show, we truly believe he was deliberately getting us a ton of votes by putting us down every week, and in particular by insulting the Scots slightly, which obviously would be bringing in a lot of money for the show through everyone voting to prove him wrong!'

In the end, The MacDonald Brothers left the series in week eight. Far from being embittered by Cowell's treatment of them, they recall some enjoyable experiences with him when the cameras weren't rolling and remain appreciative of what he did for them. 'He was very pleasant and respectful to us backstage and off camera,' Craig insists, smiling. 'We certainly have the utmost respect for him and are for ever grateful for the start he and his show gave us in the recording industry.'

There are, however, contestants who have been deeply disappointed by the aftermath of their *X Factor* experience. Even some of the more successful graduates of the show warn future contestants that it's not all rosy. 'They'll realize quickly,' 2005 runner-up Andy Abraham told *The Sunday Times*, 'that the industry doesn't want them.' When series one winner Steve Brookstein parted ways with Cowell, he says that he was given the cold shoulder wherever he turned. 'I was basically shunned by the industry,' he says. 'No serious management would touch me because they've all got connections with Simon.'

As they prepared for the *X Factor* final, Cowell and his fellow judges put on a live performance of their own. He, Osbourne and Walsh joined Sir Elton John on stage during a special charity performance of the hit musical *Billy Elliot*. In one hilarious scene, they played the part of a judging panel. Osbourne told the Elliot character to 'stand on the X', while Cowell said – before the dancer had even performed – 'it's a no from me'. Then, for the final curtain call, the three judges returned to the stage dressed in tutus. The evening was held in aid of ThePlace2Be, a childrens' charity, and it proved an enjoyable night away from official *X Factor* duties for Cowell.

Ultimately the final of that series came down to a face-off between beautiful north Londoner Leona Lewis and eighteen-year-old Liverpudlian Ray Quinn, both of whom were Cowell acts. When the other remaining singer – Ben Mills, who was being mentored by Osbourne – was voted out at the end of the semi-final, Cowell was insufferably smug as he reminded the world that the final would be contested by two of his acts. There was little doubt that the enormously talented Lewis would win – even her opponent seemed to think as much. 'Leona and I have come all the way through boot-camp and Miami, and I knew that she would go all the way and be in the final,' said Quinn, 'but I never thought I would. To be able to share it with her is amazing. I feel so good about it.' He sang crooning tunes 'Fly Me To The Moon', 'That's Life' (with Westlife) and 'My Way'. Meanwhile, Lewis brought the house down with 'I Will Always Love You', 'All By Myself' and 'A Million Love Songs' (with Take That).

Cowell regularly reminded viewers that both finalists were mentored by him. This was a great riposte to the accusations aired earlier in the live finals from Walsh that Cowell hadn't spent enough time with his acts. At the end of the evening, Lewis and Quinn held hands centre stage as the winner was announced. Quinn's demeanour showed he fully expected Lewis to be named the winner, and she was. She sang the winners' single, 'A Moment Like This', which had first been recorded in series one of *American Idol* by Kelly Clarkson. As he proudly watched Lewis sing, Cowell moved beyond the pantomime smugness of earlier in the evening and took true pride in what this series of the *X Factor* had achieved. In Lewis, it was widely felt, he had a real potential superstar on his hands. Already he had in mind that she could work well in America and go on to become a hugely successful international recording artist. 'Some people wait a lifetime, for a moment like this,' she sang and the words could just as easily apply to her mentor, Cowell.

Lewis has gone on to surpass all expectations. In the wake of the show, on 20 December 2006, she released her debut single, 'A Moment Like This', which sold 571,000 copies in its first week. It was a staggering figure – more than the rest of the top forty combined – and it immediately became the most downloaded song of the year, as well as scooping an Ivor Novello award. Her second single 'Bleeding Love' went to number one in thirty different countries and her first album, *Spirit*, fared extraordinarily well, reaching number one in numerous countries, including America, where Cowell had worked hard to break her, including her as a guest performer on *American Idol*. In the autumn of 2008, Lewis set a new record for the fastest selling download-only release in the UK with her cover of Snow Patrol's song 'Run', which sold 69,244 in just two days. When she performed the song as a returning singer on *The X Factor*, Cowell's pride in her was palpable, and he seemed close to tears as he praised her.

In March 2006, a report in the *Sunday People* claimed that Cowell had bought Lewis a mansion in America with his own money. 'Simon thinks she is absolutely amazing, so he wanted to treat her,' a source told the newspaper. 'He's so pleased with how hard she works and what a massive success she's become. Leona's a homely girl and isn't at all flash, so Simon got the idea to buy her something practical she would use. He sees a bright future for her. He thinks she can become a global star like Shirley Bassey or Whitney Houston.' Cowell and Lewis have a great rapport, leading to speculation in some quarters that their relationship is more than professional. Lewis denies this, although she can understand his allure to members of the opposite sex. 'He's really charming in real life. He's a real gentleman and really supportive – he's very popular with the ladies,' she told the *Mirror*, while adding, 'I didn't fancy him; he's old enough to be my dad! But a lot of my friends who met him thought he was so lovely.'

In 2007, Cowell had further plans for the *Got Talent* franchise, which he was confident would eclipse anything he had achieved before. He had plans to launch the franchise in the United Kingdom and then across the planet, cementing his global business empire. First, though, he had a storm to weather after something he did on *American Idol* was wildly misinterpreted. For a long, horrible day, it was feared that a savage misunderstanding threatened to derail his continuing journey to American superstardom.

# CHAPTER EIGHT

# THE TALENTED MR COWELL

On 17 April 2007, a young student called Seung-Hui Cho went on a killing spree at Virginia Polytechnic Institute and State University. He killed thirty-two people and wounded many more before turning the gun on himself. It was the deadliest shooting rampage in US history and naturally it stunned America and the world. President George W. Bush said the US was 'shocked and saddened', adding, 'Schools should be places of safety, sanctuary and learning. When that sanctuary is violated, the impact is felt in every American classroom and every American community.' The nation was in mourning.

That evening, during the live *American Idol* show, contestant Chris Richardson of Chesapeake, Virginia, followed his performance by saying, 'My heart and prayers go out to Virginia Tech. I have a lot of friends over there... be strong.' As he said these words, the camera was on Cowell, who was rolling his eyes and raising his eyebrows. Immediately, a viewer uploaded that clip of the show onto the Internet and headlined it, 'Cowell's shocking snub to Virginia.' As is often the case with the worldwide web, the clip was quickly forwarded and watched by millions, and many people concluded that Cowell was rolling his eyes in reference to Richardson's tribute to the people of Virginia. Soon the mainstream media leapt on the news, and the story was in danger of running out of control. Even Cowell's pal and colleague Piers Morgan, watching the clip at home in Britain on *GMTV* the following morning, could understand why people who didn't know Cowell as well as he did would misinterpret what they were seeing.

The scandal was potentially lethal for Cowell's US career. He had worked hard for years to strike the perfect balance in his public image: that of a straight-talking judge, but one with a heart and a sense of restraint. Yes, he was direct with contestants who he thought hadn't performed well, very direct on occasion, but despite his Mr Nasty tag, nobody could accuse him of being genuinely nasty and the sort of man who, as America mourned a national tragedy, would mock the dead. However, this was exactly the accusation that some made as the scandal spun out of control. Cowell had to act quickly, and he did, by explaining what had really happened on the following evening's results show.

'There seems to be a bit of confusion over what happened,' said Seacrest, opening the way for Cowell's explanation. 'Just a bit,' agreed Cowell. 'Look, I wouldn't normally comment on a press story about me or *American Idol*. But last night on the show Chris and I got into quite a heated debate about singing through your nose, and after I'd finished talking [to him] I was talking to Paula, and unfortunately I didn't hear Chris mention the people of Virginia. So on camera, I gave a look, but I was giving a look to Paula. I just want to absolutely set the record straight: I didn't hear what Chris was saying. I may not be the nicest person in the world, but I would never ever, ever, ever disrespect those families or victims, and I felt it was important to set the record straight.' Footage was then shown of the incident with Cowell and Abdul's microphones audible, which confirmed that they were discussing the contestant's nasal delivery when Cowell rolled his eyes.

It wasn't the first time a Cowell gesture on *American Idol* had been misinterpreted. In 2004, during the third series of the show, he exchanged words with contestant Fantasia Barrino over her dress sense, culminating in her telling him, 'Simon, you don't know class!' He then rested his head on his hands with his middle finger to the fore, leading to speculation that he was secretly flipping the bird at either Barrino, or perhaps even his fellow judge Abdul. And the previous year, when he rubbed his eye with his middle finger, some had wondered if he was directing the gesture at host Ryan Seacrest. The episodes became known as 'fingergate', much to Cowell's amusement. However, the Virginia misunderstanding had amused nobody. Executive producer Ken Warwick confirmed to the BBC that Cowell was 'mortified' by the accusations. 'He would be the biggest fool on television if he did that. And he's not a fool, believe me,' Warwick added. Fellow producer Nigel Lythgoe also came out in Cowell's defence. 'This is a sad time for everyone, so it is especially disheartening that a quick camera cutaway could have been misinterpreted,' he said. Cowell confirmed to pal Piers Morgan that he had been taken by surprise by the whole scandal. 'It was terrifying!' he told him. 'I didn't even know what I was supposed to have done, and suddenly the whole of America is going bonkers!' Fortunately, he handled the issue sensibly and the accusation against him was quickly dropped and forgotten.

Meanwhile, it was time for Cowell to start work on the second series of *America's Got Talent*. When Morgan arrived in America to film, he was given another reminder of Cowell's focused, ambitious nature. 'This is a really important time,' Cowell told Morgan as the latter recalled in his book *God Bless America*. 'A lot of shows start well in America and then disappear without trace. I don't want that happening with *Talent*, so give it everything you've got in the next few weeks to build on the success of the first series. We've got to get the ratings up.' To help this, Cowell had replaced series one presenter Philbin with the legendary broadcasting star Jerry Springer and Brandy with *X Factor* hell-raiser Sharon Osbourne. Her inclusion was a typically contentious move by Cowell, since she and Morgan had fallen out in the recent past over some comments he had made about her, all of which guaranteed that sparks would fly, both on and off camera. Indeed, sparks flew even before they went on air together. In his memoir, Morgan recalls a memorable dinner at the ultra-fashionable Mr Chow's restaurant in Beverly Hills, where Osbourne made it clear she hadn't forgiven Morgan, shrieking at him, 'Shut up, you middle-class fucking pillock,' to the astonishment of their fellow diners. She then added, 'You're Simon Cowell without the talent or the fucking class, darling.' When the show began, they continued to bicker, with Osbourne threatening to walk out at one point because of a comment Morgan made to a nine-year-old contestant. Cowell smiled the smile of an arch manipulator who had successfully started a conflict that made compelling viewing.

At the end of the series, the act that finished first was ventriloquist/impressionist Terry Fator from Dallas, Texas. The true winner, though, as always, was Cowell.

Cowell had another victory soon after when he beat the BBC to the rights for the talent show search for the two leads of a new production of the musical *Grease*. 'In my opinion, *Grease* is the best musical on the planet,' he said at the launch of the show. 'These two parts will be the most sought-after roles in the West End. It will work beautifully for us as a reality show. There will be a lot of twists.' Perhaps the most unexpected twist was how poorly the show, on which Cowell was executive producer, performed. '*Grease is the Word* isn't going as well as I had hoped,' Cowell admitted during the show's run. 'It has been slaughtered by the critics and rightly so. It's far too similar to our other formats.' The cause wasn't helped by the press leaks about the identity of one of the finalists weeks before the finals began. Cowell took the disappointment on the chin, and his dismay over *Grease is the Word* was eased when he sold the *Got Talent* franchise to forty new countries, including Russia, Greece, Israel and Kazakhstan. It was a deal that took his personal fortune to an estimated £200 million, according to the *Daily Mail*, which is always a good way to cushion the blow of a professional disappointment!

After *Grease*, it was time to introduce the *Got Talent* genre to British television where, of course, it had originally been intended to start, before Paul O'Grady's defection to Channel 4 forced Cowell to change his plans and start the franchise in America. For the presenters for *Britain's Got Talent*, Cowell turned to the presenters of *Pop Idol* – Ant and Dec, who he has described as the two most talented people he has ever worked with. On the UK show, Cowell chose to come out from behind the cameras and be a judge, and he hoped to have David Hasselhoff and Girls Aloud star Cheryl Cole alongside him – only they turned him down. In Cole's case it was because she doubted her ability to be nasty. 'I don't think I can be cruel to anyone, really,' she told the *Sun*. Perhaps Cowell's harsh comments about her in 2003, when she took part in *Popstars: The Rivals*, were still ringing in her ears. At the time Cowell had told the *Sun*, 'The Geordie girl, she's crap. I remember seeing her last audition and she couldn't sing a note in tune. I'm amazed she got through.' In the end, he hired Piers Morgan and actress Amanda Holden for *Britain's Got Talent*. The format was essentially the same as *America's Got Talent*, with open auditions held across the UK. There, the judges saw the good, the bad and the ridiculous and narrowed the field down ready for the live shows, which would be filmed in June 2007. The auditions saw the eccentrics of Britain turn up and perform everything from mime to dance, songs and magic tricks. Cowell loved every minute of it. Here, he felt, was a show that not only entertained, but celebrated what was great about Britain.

The live shows were filmed at the award-winning Fountain Studios in Wembley, which had been opened in 1994. It was the same venue that had been used for the live shows of *Pop Idol* and *The X Factor*. Piers Morgan recalls in his memoir a cheeky moment from Cowell backstage one day. Cowell arrived before Holden went into make-up, and seeing his fellow judge, said, 'Amanda, I don't mean to be rude but can you please make sure you're always fully made up when I see you. Something dies inside me when I see you without your make-up on.' It's clearly not just the contestants who fall victim to his naughty sense of humour!

As the series neared the grand finale, Cowell began to feel nervous. Behind the scenes he paced up and down the corridors outside the dressing rooms alone, smoking and looking tensely at the floor. Morgan approached him and asked if he was feeling anxious. 'God yes,' replied Cowell. 'This is where you earn your money.' In front of a live studio audience and ten million television viewers, the opening live shows were a success, despite Cowell suffering from an intense migraine on the night of the semi-final. He also had to face the metaphorical headache of having two acts removed from the competition after embarrassing press reports revealed that one was on the sex offenders' register for an offence committed in 2005, and a band composed of drag queens were also prostitutes. 'Britain's Got Perverts', was among the distressing newspaper headlines Cowell woke up to one morning.

An act that had been eliminated for entirely different reasons was young street dancer George Sampson. The thirteen-year-old turned up to the auditions on the advice of his dance teacher, and wowed Cowell. 'One word,' he said at the act's conclusion, 'Brilliant. Seriously, brilliant. You are a phenomenal dancer.' The crowd agreed, cheering on Sampson's inspired performance. Morgan and Holden were also impressed, so he went through to the next round. However, there his journey ended after Cowell's fellow judges deemed he wasn't ready for the live shows. It wasn't the last that *Britain's Got Talent*, or Britain, would hear of Sampson.

The live final, on 17 June 2007, was contested by crooked-teethed opera singer Paul Potts and six-year-old cute singer Connie Talbot. Both acts were great on the night, and Cowell's enjoyment and pride was palpable. As both singers stood centre stage, waiting for the results of the public vote, a producer whispered the name of the winner in Cowell's ear. He leant over to Holden and Morgan and whispered, 'Connie, by a landslide.' Both were shocked as they had expected Potts to win. Ant and Dec then announced that the winner of *Britain's Got Talent* was... Paul Potts. As Holden and Morgan turned to Cowell, he winked at them cheekily and burst out laughing.

After the show, Cowell took some key colleagues to the Dorchester Hotel, where champagne corks popped and laughter filled the air. 'That was the best show I've ever worked on,' he told his team. He was to work on many more, as he had recently inked a reported twenty-million-pound deal to appear on three more series of *The X Factor*.

With his television empire growing, the talented Mr Cowell was beginning to approach national treasure status in the hearts and minds of the British public. He took a step closer to this when he appeared at the Concert For Diana at the recently re-opened Wembley Stadium on 1 July 2007. Bringing *American Idol* colleagues Randy Jackson and Ryan Seacrest with him, he took to the stage to plentiful applause from the 90,000-strong audience. He took time to praise Princes William and Harry, who had arranged the concert in tribute to their late mother, who had died in a Paris car crash ten years previously. 'You've put on one heck of a show,' he told them from the stage. 'In years to come, if you ever get tired of running the country, you can come and work for me producing TV shows.' This wasn't the first time that Cowell had praised Prince William. At the launch of the second series of

*Pop Idol* he had said, 'Prince William would make a great pop idol. He's got the looks and class of a true star. 'I'd love to see him sing a ballad reflecting on the troubles in his life.' Back at the Wembley concert, Prince William was, reportedly, awe-struck by the nod of approval from Cowell, who then introduced the next act on the bill, Nelly Furtado. She's 'one of the biggest stars in the world', he told the audience. He is quite at home in such a role: the previous year he had introduced American TV personality Dick Clark at the Emmys.

Such were the benefits of his remarkably swift ascent to fame. At the start of 2001, his only experience of television was as a contestant on *Sale of the Century*. Yet as 2008 dawned, he was at the top of the broadcasting ladder in both Britain and America as a judge and as a producer. His shows had been sold around the world and he was one of the richest, most famous men on the planet. Television development producer Jonathan Sacerdoti has watched Cowell's rise with interest and assessed why he is ahead of the pack. 'He's not just startlingly honest but also very insightful,' says Sacerdoti, who has worked for some of Britain's top independent production companies, including Endemol and Shine, developing everything from game shows to reality TV shows. 'When you see that many rubbish acts, day after day, one after the other, as often as he does, it must be quite hard to pinpoint what's bad about them. He's always very clear about it and very honest.'

Sacerdoti has worked at a company that crossed paths with Cowell. 'Everyone I know who's met him in the TV world says he is exactly the same in person as he is on television, but nicer,' he smiles. 'He's very good with people, like *really* good with people.

We were developing lots of programmes for a co-production with his company. Some colleagues went out for lunch to discuss stuff, and when the boss came back he said, "Everybody stops and talks to him, everybody wants to come and say hi. He's totally charming with them all." He said no other famous people he'd ever met had been like that with the public. Most people get a bit snotty about it and want them to go away. But Cowell was really charming to everybody who came their way.'

That genuine sincerity has, Sacerdoti believes, prevented Cowell from making a mistake that's all too common among on-screen television personalities. 'Television has this amazing tendency to make people turn into a caricature of themselves,' he says. 'Everyone does it. Jamie Oliver started out as an everyman sort of chav, but then became the cheekie-chappie who says "pukka" every two minutes. He became his own caricature because that was his hype, and I don't think Cowell believes his own hype. I think if you watch Cowell in the first series of *Pop Idol* and then watch him now, it's the same bloke. The teeth have got whiter, the tan's a bit better, but it's the same guy. I don't think he believes, or gets caught up in, his own hype.' It's a view that Cowell has often said he shares.

Famous British journalist Julie Burchill also admires Cowell. Like Cowell, she has built a career around being straight-talking and appeared in Channel 4's 2003 Worst Britons poll, as did Cowell. 'He's a sentimental sadist,' she purrs, adding with a wicked smile, 'my very favourite sort of man.' She says she identifies with his combination of tough-talking and charm. 'The trick is not to be nasty for the sake of it, but because you really don't have a choice – because you are literally incapable of being a hypocrite. It's an unusual and charming quality,' she says. 'I admire his complete and utter honesty about his ambition in an age of showbusiness hypocrisy. Everybody else pretends they became rich and famous "accidentally" and would give it all up tomorrow for an ordinary life. They're fooling no one and they show themselves up as being such tragic tools when they say so.' He is, she argues, 'the female Julie Burchill'. Adding, 'If I was thirty years younger and three stone lighter... well, we'd be very compatible.'

There was hype aplenty surrounding Cowell as his fame and fortune rose ever higher. It's a remarkable story, one that a fiction writer would resist writing for fear of lacking credibility. His next television project was set to be a fictional one that would have seen him join forces with Shed Productions to make *Rock Rivals*, a drama based around a television talent show. In the series, an egotistical record producer called Mal Faith (played by Sean Gallagher) constantly bickers with and cheats on his wife (played by Michelle Collins). The tabloids quickly speculated that Mal might be based on Cowell himself. However, Cowell didn't end up working on *Rock Rivals*. A production source revealed, 'Simon's team felt that some of the storylines were too outlandish and over-fictionalized and Simon didn't want his name associated with it.' Cowell flatly denied there were any hard feelings and told the same newspaper, 'I'm sure it will be a great drama, but my company is not producing it.'

It wasn't the first time a fictional character was believed to be based on Cowell. In 2006, a movie called *American Dreamz*, directed by Paul Weitz, featured Hugh Grant playing a mean judge on a television pop talent show. Inevitable comparisons with Cowell were made, but Grant dismissed the connection. 'I have met Simon Cowell at a couple of parties, but I don't know him at all,' the British actor told a press conference in 2006. 'This part is not particularly based on him, aside from the fact that I am a judge on a talent show that is massively popular and I'm very cruel. There the resemblance stops. The part really is a creation of Paul Weitz and actually, in part, his warped vision of me.'

Whether Grant's character was based on Cowell or not, he was definitely the inspiration for Calvin Simms, a character in Ben Elton novel published in 2006. *Chart Throb* is the story of a pop talent show run by manipulative genius Simms. When Cowell read the novel, far from taking offence, he laughed and phoned Elton to praise him. The two men have since become friends, and a shared love of banter is just one of their common characteristics. When Elton appeared on *This is Your Life*, he said, 'For Simon, masturbation is not about self-abuse, it's about fidelity.' Cowell roared with laughter at the joke. No wonder he was in such good humour: he remains one of the few stars to have had more than one episode of *This is Your Life* devoted to him.

Not only has Cowell been the inspiration for fictional characters, he's proved himself perfectly capable of creating drama of his own on his talent shows, and much of this has revolved around his tendency to toy with the other judges on the panel. For the fourth series of *The X Factor*, Cowell decided to drop Walsh from the line-up and introduce two new judges, choreographer Brian Friedman and Australian pop star Dannii Minogue, sister of the legendary Kylie. However, soon into the filming of the first auditions, Cowell decided it wasn't working, removed Friedman from the panel and brought Walsh back in his place. 'I was devastated when I was axed and didn't even hesitate when I was asked back,' the

Irishman said in the official *X Factor* book. It was speculated in the tabloid press that the entire drama surrounding Walsh being axed and reinstated was a pre-arranged plot by Cowell to create publicity.

However, the introduction of Minogue caused the most controversy. Cowell had watched her as a judge on *Australia's Got Talent* and said, 'I want that girl for *The X Factor*.' She was thrilled to be invited and enjoyed being part of the show. She told an interviewer for the *Mirror*, 'I'm quite fluttery with happiness. I've finally been accepted as me. It's a fantastic opportunity, for once, not to be compared with Kylie. At last, I've found my own slot.' Less fluttery with happiness about the Aussie's introduction was fellow judge Osbourne, who reportedly had numerous off-air clashes with the new, younger judge. Osbourne told the *Evening Standard*, 'She [Dannii] knows she's there because of her looks, not because of her contribution to the music industry. She's younger, she's better-looking, Simon wants her and he doesn't want me – thank God.'

Minogue did little to calm the tension when she told reporters that she felt 'younger and prettier' sitting alongside Osbourne. Cowell then stoked the row further by saying of the two female judges, 'When I sit next to one, the other sulks. I have to try to give each one equal attention. You know, girls can be very catty and it's been very interesting watching how another woman has affected the dynamic of the group.' It did indeed seem that Cowell was attracted to Minogue, who he described as 'mysterious and sexy', adding, 'she doesn't know how sexy she is'. Soon, perhaps inevitably, rumours started to fly that Cowell and Minogue were more than just colleagues, particularly after a photographer caught the pair holding hands. Cowell denied the rumours, as did Minogue, who said – to raised eyebrows – that she fancied 'nerdy guys like [*Private Eye* editor and *Have I Got News For You* captain] Ian Hislop'.

However, Minogue proved to be a good judge on the show. Luke Bayer, then fourteen, was one of Minogue's acts until the judges' houses stage, when she sent him home. He recalls his earlier encounters with Cowell with the most warmth. Having auditioned with the song 'Maggie May' first time round, he was asked by Cowell to return with a new song. He duly did, singing 'You Raise Me Up'. Cowell told him 'We're friends now, right?' and then announced that he was voting 'no'. Despite the fact that the other judges put him through, Bayer was disappointed. 'I was absolutely gutted because I really wanted Simon's approval,' says Bayer during a break from his A-level revision. 'This made me more determined when I went to boot-camp. I knew I had to do a good performance to get through and I took the feedback Simon gave me and worked on it. Simon seemed to like my boot-camp a lot better than my first one which I was really happy about!' Again, it seems that it's Cowell's endorsement alone that really counts with the contestants.

But what was Cowell really like with the contestants when the cameras weren't rolling? 'I thought Simon was really nice,' says Bayer, who hasn't ruled out another crack at *The X Factor* in the future. 'He seemed very genuine and friendly throughout all the audition process, and off camera too which was cool. I also went to watch a live show in the television studio on 1 December 2007, and Simon came over to me in one of the breaks and spoke to my mum and I to ask us how we were and have a little chat. He was really cool; he was very polite and not mean or scary at all!' As with Manson in series one of *Pop Idol*, we see in Bayer's memories a division between the on- and off-screen Cowell, and a tendency for him to charm the mothers of contestants.

Bayer was sent home by Minogue, but another boy in his category went on to win the fourth series of *X Factor* in 2007. Retail sales assistant Leon Jackson earned comparisons with jazz singer Michael Bublé on the show, and even covered 'Home', a Bublé track, during one of the live shows. (During his feedback, Walsh was quick to point out to the millions of viewers that his and Cowell's band Westlife were about to release the same song.) Jackson, from West Lothian in Scotland, duetted with Kylie Minogue on the night of the final and went on to beat the favourite, Welshman Rhydian Roberts. 'It's not real,' said the stunned eighteen-year-old as he was crowned winner. Bookmakers shared his surprise, with Ladbrokes saying it was 'the biggest shock in the history of reality TV betting'. Jackson's debut single 'When You Believe' went to number one, but he has since fared modestly. In November 2008 his single 'Creative' peaked at number ninety-four, and in March 2009 he was dropped by Sony BMG. He forms a dramatic contrast with the winner the previous year, Leona Lewis, and his case was more reminiscent of series one winner Steve Brookstein. It was proof that Cowell couldn't win them all, but his success rate was to bounce back with another sensational winner the following year in series five.

Niki Evans, who finished fourth in series four, warmly recalls her encounters with Cowell. Some months before filming for the series began, her father died. While going through his belongings she discovered he had sent off for an application form for the show, but had died before he could hand it to her. Consequently, this moving story was an ever-present feature of her X *Factor* journey. However, she disputes that Cowell was responsible for this. Quite the opposite was the case, she says. One week Evans, who was being mentored by Walsh, was asked to sing 'Dance With My Father' again.

'The prospect made me feel uncomfortable,' she says over coffee in a West End café, a stone's throw from the theatre where she is now the leading lady in *Blood Brothers*. 'I said, "I don't like it, I can't sing it without getting really emotional and crying my eyes out. I don't want to be going to pieces on a stage in front of twelve million people." It was very raw but I was being heavily encouraged to sing the song. I phoned Cowell and said, "I can't do this, it's too painful. I've had to see my dad dead in a fucking coffin, this is real for me, it's not a story," and he said, "Fine, don't do it. Don't even think about it again. Niki, darling, put it out of your head."'

'It's not Simon pushing the sob stories,' she says emphatically. 'If he can see you're personally hurting then he puts a stop to it instantly. He doesn't want to squash people.' She was very nearly crushed during the filming of one of her VTs – the short videos shown before a contestant's live performance – towards the end of the contest. She was taken, against her better instincts, to be filmed at her father's graveside where she became enormously emotional. 'It broke my fucking heart, I couldn't even talk,' she says. 'Simon saw this piece of footage and went fucking mental. He said, "You don't do that to people. Don't fucking crucify people like that." He made one of the production team personally phone me and apologize. He ordered them never to push me that far again. I can't tell you how big his heart is.'

A combination of the pressure of the show, her grief over the loss of her father, the fact that she was hundreds of miles away from her children and that she was suffering with a cold, meant Evans regularly needed encouragement. Although he wasn't mentoring her category, it was Cowell who was the warmest, she says, adding that the legacy of that encouragement continues to this day. 'I was a mess, I really was. But he kept saying, "Niki, we really like you. Niki, we really like you. You're better than you think you are." He's very personal and encouraging. Look at me now, I'm a leading lady in the West End, and before I met Simon Cowell I would never have had the confidence to do that.' She laughs as she recalls another aspect of Cowell's personality. 'The only thing is he is a total diva,' she says. 'But he does it in such a funny way you've got to forgive him for it. He knows he can click his fingers and get what he wants.' A generous diva, too. When she went for dinner with a friend of Cowell's a short while after she was eliminated from *The X Factor*, she was told by the waiter that Cowell had phoned through with his credit card number and paid the bill. 'To me that sums him up,' she says.

Daniel de Bourg was a finalist in the same series as Evans, and he echoes her assessment of Cowell. 'Simon's a very intelligent man,' insists de Bourg while taking a break from a songwriting session. 'He is the puppet master and he certainly pulls the strings. He's a nice guy, though. Not nasty at all off screen. He just knows what he wants and goes and gets it. I have a lot of respect for him.'

Series four was to be Osbourne's last series as an *X Factor* judge, and Cowell's choice for her replacement was to cause just as much of a stir as the introduction of Minogue. Cheryl Cole of Girls Aloud had found fame through reality television talent show *Popstars: The Rivals.* Therefore, when she was confirmed as an *X Factor* judge for series five – overcoming her earlier qualms about passing judgement on others – it marked something of a milestone in the genre's history. Simon had wanted her to judge the first series of *Britain's Got Talent*, but she had turned him down. However when Cole's *X Factor* chance came along, she took it, and Minogue found she was no longer the youngest face on the panel. Soon she was complaining the producers were biased towards Cole. Minogue didn't seem entirely happy beside Cole on the panel and it was not long before she was rowing with Walsh, too. Once more, by mixing up the judging panel Cowell had created tensions that guaranteed regular coverage of the show in the press.

Cowell also shook things up by introducing a new presenter from series four onwards. Out went Kate Thornton – who had worked with Cowell since the first series of *Pop Idol* – and in came *Big Brother* presenter Dermot O'Leary. Thornton was furious about the decision and the way she was informed. 'I'll never talk to Simon again,' she stormed. 'He fired me to create headlines without even telling me beforehand when we had been good friends. I wouldn't watch the show now because it would be like seeing your ex-boyfriend with his new girlfriend. You don't have feelings for them any more, but you don't want to see it.' Whether or not headlines were Cowell's motivation for playing musical chairs with the judging and presenting line-ups, he certainly grabbed them, and those headlines helped guarantee viewers. It's not only in Britain that Cowell is perceived as playing these media-manipulation games. When singer/songwriter Kara DioGuardi was introduced as a fourth judge on *American Idol*,

Cowell admitted to *OK!* magazine that he hoped to stir up a feud between her and Paula Abdul. The elder female judge said he didn't have a hope. 'That's just Simon trying to conjure up his shenanigans,' she told the same magazine. 'Kara and I are good friends.'

Television critic Julia Raeside insists that all these headlines are exactly what Cowell is aiming for. 'It's very clever,' says Raeside, who writes for *The Guardian* and *Radio Times*. 'From Louis Walsh leaving and then being reinstated on *X Factor*, to stories about which female judge is scared about losing their job on *X Factor* to Amanda Holden worrying about her job on *Britain's Got Talent*, and the whole Kelly Brook episode when she came in and was sent out again [in series three]. He knows how to keep our interest. It's not just about what happens in the shows, it's the whole soap opera surrounding them.'

Raeside adds that Cowell has become more than merely a television personality. 'He's a brand,' she says. 'By some miracle, after eight years of him being the same person, the public haven't got bored of him yet. I'm not sure why, it must be some form of low-level hypnosis.' As for her fellow broadsheet television critics, she says they have learned to live with Cowell's popularity, if not entirely enjoy it. 'I suppose the first series of *Pop Idol* was the one that got the most credibility from us, because in terms of manipulation it was probably the most unblemished of all the shows,' she says. 'He was very clear that he wanted Gareth and not Will to win and he didn't get his way. Since then, there has always been a sense that he's an arch manipulator and that he creates a whole soap opera around the shows he is involved in. That is something he started and now every other talent show on every other channel has copied. Take *Strictly Come Dancing* as an example: you simply wouldn't get the judges squabbling and pretending to dislike each other the way they do if Cowell hadn't introduced that on his shows. He started all that.'

The headlines Cowell created kept viewers watching shows like *The X Factor*. Those viewers watched as series three reject Alexandra Burke returned for a second attempt at the show in series five. She came back an improved person in every sense: looks, vocals and attitude, and with Cole as her mentor, she made it all the way to the final. Along the way, Cowell mercilessly mocked Walsh, who had rejected her in series three. After one performance during the live finals, Cowell tried to contain a smirk as he reminded Burke, 'Louis nearly wrecked your life three years ago. You needed a break; he crushed your dreams.' Her dreams were realized when she was crowned *X Factor* winner of series five. The show had pulled off an unlikely trick by discovering an artist who had the potential to eclipse the success of the previous series' champion Leona Lewis. A total of 105,000 copies of her winners' single 'Hallelujah' were sold on the first day of release, which beat Lewis's equivalent figure of 85,000. Burke has since signed a three-million-dollar, five-album US record deal with Epic Records.

Cowell actually launched two new careers with series five of *X Factor*. His decision to appoint Cheryl Cole to the judging panel proved a masterstroke, turning her from a pop star into a television personality. 'I have always wanted Cheryl to be part of one of these programmes,' he said at the launch press conference for the show. 'I was first impressed by her when she was taking part in *Celebrity Apprentice* and she came to me and charmed me out of a very big cheque.' Having been turned down by Cole when he offered her a place on the judging panel for *Britain's Got Talent*, Cowell had finally got his girl for *The X Factor*.

The tension between Cole and Minogue gave the show a new dimension, and Cole proved to be televisual gold. Cowell now has plans to launch her as a television star in America, too. He believes that as long as he can overcome the hurdle of obtaining a visa for her – she has a minor conviction on her record for assault occasioning actual bodily harm following an incident in a Guildford nightclub in 2003 – he can make her even more famous than Piers Morgan in the States. He has already instructed a firm of experts in Miami to thrash out an agreement that will overcome the visa issue. He has also toyed with the idea of trying to break Ant and Dec in the United States. If he can make Piers Morgan a success over there, Ant and Dec should have a good chance of making it.

Meanwhile, 2008 saw Cowell continue to show that despite his enormous ambition, he retains a generous and caring side. However, unlike his secretive work for hospices such as The Chase, this time he declared his generosity in front of millions of American television viewers on *Oprah*. Cowell was a guest on the chat show to promote *X Factor* winner Leona Lewis in the US when he watched a video in which a couple called Randy and Amy Stoen spoke of the torment they were going through due to their daughter Madelaine's cancer. Their three-year-old had been diagnosed with a rare form of cancer, called alveolar rhabdomyosarcoma, which required extensive treatment that involved lots of travel and a major financial burden for her parents. When the parents came onto the set, Cowell told them, 'I didn't know what to do in this situation, other than to do something which I hope will help your situation. I know that you're having problems with your mortgage. As of this afternoon your mortgage has been paid off.' The couple were overcome by Cowell's generosity, as was Winfrey, who gave him a high-five in honour of his gesture.

Later on the show, Cowell revealed that he planned to do more than just pay off their $162,000 mortgage. 'The money for me is not the important part. It's when you see that film and that little girl. I said to the parents, "It doesn't stop there. If there are any problems, I'm her guardian angel now."' He got positive headlines across the globe for his generosity and his Mr Nasty tag seemed a distant memory. 'Mr Nice: Cowell Pays Off Couple's Mortgage', sang *The Independent*. 'It's No More Mr Nasty as Cowell Becomes Guardian Angel', said the *Sydney Morning Herald*. 'Cowell Donates £81,000 to Young Cancer Patient', reported *China Daily*. Acts of huge generosity were, he told Winfrey, a relatively new activity for him, and he attributed his new-found hobby to her influence. 'I never knew that doing good could feel so good. It's taken me forty-eight years. I credit you with this.' America naturally warmed even more to Cowell in the wake of this public altruism.

Back in the United Kingdom, Cowell's charity continued when he attended the annual Norwood Dinner, which raise funds for thousands of Jewish children and families with learning difficulties and social problems. During his speech at the event, he revealed that he had only three years previously learned that his father was Jewish. 'I always suspected it but... I was delighted. Somebody phoned me and said, "Did you know that?" And I said, "No," but I was happy.' Zeddy Lawrence, the editor of *Jewish News* and a veteran of hundreds of charity bashes, was at the event and was pleasantly surprised by Cowell's behaviour on the night. 'In my line of work I'm constantly invited to big charity events,' beams Lawrence. 'There are often celebrity guest speakers at these events and I can say without a doubt that Simon was the friendliest and most approachable such guest I have ever encountered. We were warned beforehand not to approach him with photograph requests, but in reality he happily spent the whole evening speaking to strangers and having his photograph taken with them.

'He seemed genuinely pleased and almost honoured that people wanted to speak to him. I don't know how he found the time to eat because all night he was graciously speaking to guests and having his photograph taken with them on mobile phones. He was the most genuine guest at a charity event I've ever witnessed.' Numerous people attest to Cowell's graciousness with autograph hunters and members of the public who approach him. Still in his mind, it seems, is that childhood day when Cowell met Bernard Cribbins and asked for his autograph. 'He basically told me to go away,' he explained. 'I was seven years old and I still remember that.'

Cowell is comfortable with that side of fame, but he had a brush with a less savoury side in December 2008. For some months he had noticed that whenever he arrived at a private meeting, the same mysterious motorcyclist would appear a few minutes later. How does he know where I am? wondered Cowell. So he called his security team to ask them to investigate. As part of their inquiries, they checked Cowell's cars and found a sophisticated tracking device on his £140,000 Bentley Continental.

Understandably, Cowell was shaken by this discovery. 'Simon

is completely freaked out by this. He can't believe someone has gone to so much trouble and expense to monitor his every movement. It's extremely sinister,' a source told the *Mirror*. 'He was aware that someone dressed in motorbike leathers and a crash helmet kept turning up a few minutes after he went anywhere. He couldn't work out how that person knew his movements. His security team found the tracking device under the car. It was quite sophisticated and could have been used by the security services. Simon has his suspicions as to who is responsible. He is so angry he is considering calling in the police to investigate further. It is a hassle he could do without – especially with *The X Factor* in its final stages – but it has to be done. He can't take any chances.'

Earlier in the year he had found bugging devices in the judges' room backstage at Manchester's Palace Theatre during auditions for *Britain's Got Talent*. Cowell said at the time, 'This shows the extent to which people will go to to get inside knowledge.' Both were upsetting reminders to Cowell that the fame he has acquired since first appearing on *Pop Idol* in 2001 has its disadvantages.

Cowell has long insisted that those who chase fame must accept the good and bad parts of celebrity. However, he felt that the tracking device on his car constituted a step too far, and he got his press advisor Max Clifford straight on the case. The first task was to warn the journalist who Cowell felt was responsible. 'We know who he is and we have marked his card and told him never to do anything like that again,' Clifford said. 'We have always played the game and we are not precious, but this is way beyond anything acceptable. So Carter-Ruck [libel solicitors] has sent a letter out to everybody warning them about this and making clear that it is unacceptable,' he added. 'Simon has been putting up with this for seven years, with people approaching him at all hours, and we know that we have got to have working relationships with the papers, but within acceptable boundaries.'

The increased press interest in Cowell came partly due to renewed rumours about his love life. In the wake of series five of *The X Factor*, reports began to circulate that all was far from well between him and girlfriend Terri Seymour. It had been rumoured since December 2008 that the couple were rowing over her desire to have children. It was understood that the issue had ruined their Christmas holiday in Barbados. Then, in April 2009, there was gossip that the relationship was at breaking point. Soon it was confirmed by the couple that they had decided to bring an end to their relationship. 'We've split up,' she was quoted as saying in the *Mirror*. 'It's very sad but we decided to go our separate ways. It just wasn't working out between us. There's no one else involved and we want to remain friends.'

Seymour was quick to confirm that she had gone into the relationship with her eyes open as to Cowell's views on love and family. 'I have known his thoughts on marriage and babies from the beginning,' she said. 'He doesn't want kids, full stop. But I would love to have a baby in the future, definitely.' Cowell had told the same paper in the past, 'I don't believe in marriage, certainly not in this business. The truth is that you get married and in a year or two they clean you out. It's just not going to work. It doesn't work. It changes you. That whole culture just puts you in a very weakened position.' As for children, his views on fatherhood were also well-known. He has said he has never felt a need to have another him and that he didn't want babies in the same way he wouldn't want a puppy. Indeed, the previous Christmas Seymour had told *Now* magazine of a conversation she and Cowell had had about parenthood. 'He used to tell me that if I wanted children, he'd buy me a terrapin,' she said.

The ending of Cowell's relationship with Seymour brought to an end the longest relationship he had ever had with a woman. While both parties always played down suggestions they might one day marry, it was hoped by many of Cowell's family and friends that he had finally found 'the one' who he would settle down with. Instead, as he approached his fiftieth birthday, he was single once again. As for Seymour, she has shown no signs of bitterness since the split. To all appearances she was equal to Cowell throughout their relationship, giving as good as she got when his famously sharp tongue lashed out. 'He's always critiquing me,' she said during an interview on NBC's *Extra TV* show in 2006, 'but I give him as good as he gets.' The same show was the venue for a surprising post-split interview that Cowell and Seymour gave in the wake of their break-up. The pair suggested there were no hard feelings by sitting together on camera. They joked and laughed about their relationship and break-up.

During the interview it was put to them that Cowell had 'paid-off' Seymour with £2.3 million in cash and a mansion in Beverly Hills worth the same sum. Seymour asked him, 'Did you give me five million dollars in cash?' Cowell emphatically responded, 'No! No!' Seymour laughed and told him, 'Everybody thinks you did!' and Cowell again denied it, saying, 'No, that is actually not a true story.' Cowell then grimaced and huffed: 'This is the weirdest interview I have ever done!' The pair remain in touch and have been seen dining happily at Hollywood Boulevard restaurant

Beso, which is owned by actress Eva Longoria, where fine steaks and jumbo sea scallops are among the specialities. Seymour has also been Cowell's guest at an *American Idol* live show. However, Cowell denies reports that he has tried to rekindle their relationship. He is in no hurry to find a new partner. 'I don't have enough time to go out. I quite like being single,' he told *Metro*.

That said, in the wake of his split with Seymour, Cowell gave a revealing interview to the *Daily Mail*, in which he explained that he has 'dark moods', and sometimes almost forces himself to brood, perhaps as a counterbalance to his endless professional success and the obligations that brings. 'If I went to a psychiatrist, it would be a long session,' he said. 'I've always thought that I do have a number of issues that probably need dealing with, because I am quite odd in some ways. I get very dark moods for no reason. Nothing in particular brings it on. You can be having the best time of your life and yet you're utterly and totally miserable. I get very anti-social, depressed and irritable with people. I don't have time for them. I can't make phone calls and stuff. I just sit on my own for days. I'm not sitting in a darkened room rocking. Things might have gone really well and then I torture myself. I cannot believe it. I have to find something to make me miserable.'

When Cowell does go out nowadays, it is to move in increasingly powerful circles. He was invited to a private dinner hosted by Prime Minister Gordon Brown in Downing Street. It proved to be an interesting evening, during which Cowell told fellow diners, 'I have decided to freeze myself when I die. You know, cryonics. You pay a lot of money and you get stuck in a deep freeze once you've been declared dead. Medical science is bound to work out a way of bringing us back to life in the next century or so, and I want to be available when they do. I would be doing the nation an invaluable service.' Cowell has since insisted he was joking. He was full of self-confidence that night, holding court on a range of political issues in front of the Prime Minister, including the economy and knife-crime. 'This is still a great country,' he told Brown. 'You just need to make people feel proud of it again, like we do on *Britain's Got Talent*.'

He has also dined with Brown's opposite number, the Conservative Party leader David Cameron. In June 2008 the pair spent an evening at the celebrity restaurant Cipriani, in a meeting arranged by Cameron's advisor (and former *News of the World* editor) Andy Coulson. Cameron's press team tried to play down the significance of the meeting, but Cowell's man Max Clifford was in ebulient mood when speaking to the *Daily Mail*. Clifford said, 'I am sure that someone like Simon's opinions Cameron would value because of his success over the last six or seven years. In his position it's extremely helpful to get to know someone like Simon. He is one of the most powerful men in television and music and he understands what appeals to young people – and people in general. He definitely has his finger on the pulse. People like that are extremely valuable.' Clifford added, 'Maybe David wanted to ask Simon how to crack America. Simon is the only Briton who has done so. I spoke to Simon and he said the dinner went well and that Cameron was a bright man. He said that about Gordon Brown too.' Cowell certainly seems to have conducted himself confidently during dinners with both party leaders.

One brush with the establishment that Cowell emerged from with less self-assurance came in December 2007, following the Royal Variety Performance at which *Britain's Got Talent* winner

Paul Potts had performed. As Piers Morgan reported in the *Mail on Sunday*, backstage after the show, the Queen and Prince Philip were introduced to the performers and other key guests. Morgan says that the Queen 'didn't have a clue who Cowell was, shook his hand with a bemused half smile and moved swiftly on to me'. Morgan said that what happened next left Cowell gobsmacked. 'Prince Philip asked, "You're judges, is that right?" and, pointing at Potts, added, "You sponge off him then?"' That night, as Cowell and Morgan flew back to London from Liverpool in a private jet, Morgan told Cowell, 'Perfect night. The Queen didn't know you, and Philip called you a sponger.' Morgan's report quickly aroused a denial from Buckingham Palace. In a statement, a spokesman said, 'The Duke of Edinburgh has said he does not know enough about Mr Cowell to make any sort of comment about him. Mr Cowell may have misheard the Duke. He has a very soft voice.' The spokesman added, 'The Queen doesn't ignore people. Indeed there is a photograph of the Queen shaking hands with Mr Cowell and saying hello, so we are puzzled that he felt he was ignored.'

The success enjoyed by both Paul Potts and George Sampson in the wake of their respective *Britain's Got Talent* victories was considerable. Potts's debut album *One Chance* sold over three and a half million copies, and reached the number one spot in fifteen countries. In the UK, his album outsold the entire top ten collectively in its first week of release, and he has since embarked on a successful hundred-date world tour. As for Sampson, he starred in a West End play called *Into the Hoods*, signed a deal to promote the 11–18 bank account for NatWest and released a single and DVD. There are hopes for further glory for both performers.

However, the first big story to emerge at the beginning of the third series of *Britain's Got Talent* was to prove a less happy one for the woman concerned, when Cowell decided to add a glamorous new member to the judging panel: the model and actress Kelly Brook. It was a role worth £200,000, according to *The Daily Telegraph*, but just six days into filming, he dropped her from the line-up, saying the format was not working with four judges. 'I have genuinely enjoyed working with Kelly, she is absolutely lovely and a complete professional,' he said in a statement. 'But it's become clear the format doesn't support another judge and we will never add a fourth judge to the panel.'

This wasn't enough to dampen speculation as to why she was dropped. Contestant Michael Hayter, who appeared at the Manchester auditions, alleged, 'Kelly was useless, really terrible.' The same newspaper reported speculation that hosts Ant and Dec were unhappy about Brook's inclusion on the show. Meanwhile Cowell's friend Sinitta cattily told the *Evening Standard*, 'Well, the show wasn't scripted, so she had to be herself.' Whatever the truth, it was an unhappy episode for Brook.

Brook wasn't the only woman who made an impression in series three. In fact it was a dowdy, middle-aged contestant who next grabbed the headlines, creating a story so huge it threatened to eclipse the whole series before it had really got started. When a forty-eight-year-old self-confessed woman who'd 'never been kissed' from West Lothian took to the stage at the *Britain's Got Talent* auditions she provoked sniggers from some of the audience. With her wiry grey hair, bushy grey eyebrows and generally unkempt appearance, she didn't stand out as a natural star. 'My name is Susan Boyle,' she told the panel. Asked by Cowell what her dream was, she replied, 'I'm trying to be a professional singer.' This triggered laughter and rolled eyes across the theatre, and the derision only increased when she said she wanted to be the next Elaine Page. She then sang 'I Dreamed A Dream' from *Les Miserables*, and her life changed instantly.

It was a beautiful, powerful performance of a song whose lyrics seemed perfectly suited to the occasion. Cowell's show had discovered an ugly duckling who could sing beautifully. There were smiles and applause across the hall by the time she had completed the song. On and on she sang, as the audience turned completely in her favour. Many of them were in tears. The three judges were enraptured by Boyle. At first Cowell looked stunned, but soon he broke into the most genuine huge smile television has ever seen from him. As the song ended, Boyle received the most powerful standing ovation ever known on the show and she blew a kiss to the audience. 'Without a doubt that was the biggest surprise I have had in three years on this show,' said a stunned Morgan. Holden admitted that the audience and panel had initially been against Boyle. 'No one is laughing now, that was stunning, an incredible performance,' she smiled. 'Amazing.' Holden then added that Boyle consituted a 'wake-up call'. Cowell, sensing the scale of the occasion, opted for a cheeky moment. 'Susan, I knew the minute you walked out on that stage that we were going to hear something extraordinary,' he claimed to widespread laughter, 'and I was right.' He smiled protectively at Boyle and added, 'Susan, you are a little tiger aren't you?' She replied that she didn't know about that. 'Oh you are,' said Cowell approvingly. He knew that they had found an extraordinary story in Boyle.

What happened next was astonishing. A video of Boyle's

performance was loaded onto YouTube and other video-sharing sites by excited viewers. Within seven days her online videos had generated a record-breaking eighty five and a half million views. Throughout April 2009, the number of people viewing the videos increased by around eight million each day. She was becoming an internet sensation across the planet. 'She's really the world's singer right now,' said YouTube spokeswoman Julie Supan. Her *Wikipedia* page attracted half a million views in the same seven-day period. The stage was set for Boyle to become an internationally successful artist before the show had finished and with little marketing effort expended. The people of the world were voting with their mouse clicks. Not all of this web attention was positive, however. One minute and twenty-four seconds into the YouTube clip, a girl in the audience is seen rolling her eyes at Boyle and she became dubbed 'The 1.24 girl' and subjected to a worldwide web hate campaign from Boyle supporters until the singer herself urged everyone to leave the girl alone.

The mainstream media leapt on Boyle's story and she became headline-making news around the world, featuring in *The Times of India*, Germany's *Der Spiegel*, China's Xinhua News Agency, Brazil's Zero Hora, Israel's Ynet and the Arabic-language Al Arabiya. Boyle was interviewed on many of the biggest American television shows, including CBS's *Early Show*, ABC's *Good Morning America*, NBC's *Today*, and Fox's *America's Newsroom*. Boyle also appeared via satellite on CNN's *Larry King Live*. It was an astonishing testament to the impact that Cowell's programmes can make on the world. Whatever happens in the future for Boyle, she has proved that Cowell can rock the globe with his talent shows. His influence is truly astonishing.

The scale of Cowell's influence was confirmed when he was name-checked by Barack Obama during an interview the American president gave on the influential *Tonight Show*, presented by Jay Leno on NBC. Referring to the culture in political circles in Washington DC, Obama referred to Britain's finest talent show judge. 'Well, look, we are going through a difficult time,' he said of the early days of his term. 'I welcome the challenge. You know, I ran for president because I thought we needed big changes. I do think in Washington it's a little bit like *American Idol*, except everybody is Simon Cowell.' This name-check from the most powerful man in the world was confirmation of Cowell's standing in America. Cowell was jubliant about it – it was the latest evidence of his rise to superstardom, and naturally he texted Morgan to show off. 'Hilarious, I love it!' read the message. The following week Cowell appeared on the live show and naturally was asked about Obama's comments. 'I was invited to have dinner with him last week, but wasn't available,' he said. 'He wanted to have dinner, but our diaries didn't quite match. He wanted to do eight, I wasn't free until nine.'

Cowell can afford to joke about the episode. His international influence is immense and his personal fortune estimated to be in excess of £100 million. As he turns fifty, there is no sign of him retiring to enjoy his riches. 'I'll only retire when I lose the plot,' he once told an interviewer. 'I don't need to work but I love it.' Love seems just the word to describe Cowell's relationship with work. Numerous theories have been offered for his unwillingness to marry and start a family. Perhaps more than anything the answer lies in the fact that Cowell's true love is work and success. In which case, there can be few more successful marriages in the world. The key ingredient in that success is that Cowell has always been honest to himself and others. At four years of age, when his mother asked him what he thought of her outfit, he told her she looked like a poodle. All these decades on, he is still as forthright, and we still can't get enough of him.

# BIBLIOGRAPHY

*Chart Throb*, Ben Elton, Black Swan 2006

*Darius: Sink or Swim*, Darius Danesh, Headline 2003

*God Bless America: Misadventures of a Big Mouth Brit*, Piers Morgan, Ebury Press 2009

*I Don't Mean to Be Rude, But...*, Simon Cowell with Tony Cowell, Ebury Press 2003

*I Hate to Be Rude, But... The Simon Cowell Book of Nasty Comments*, Tony Cowell, John Blake 2006

*Pop Idol: The Official Inside Story of the ITV Series*, Sian Solanas, Carlton Books 2002

*The X Factor: Access All Areas The Official Companion*, Jordan Paramor, Headline 2007

# Index

(the initials SC denote Simon Cowell)